Roses

A Gardener's Guide for the Plains and Prairies

George W. Shewchuk

Canadian Cataloguing in Publication Data
Shewchuk, G. W.
Roses

Previous ed. has title: Rose gardening on the prairies.
Includes index.
ISBN 1-55091-032-9

1. Rose culture--Prairie Provinces. 2. Roses--Varieties. I. University of Alberta. Faculty of Extension. II. Title. III. Title: Rose gardening on the prairies.
SB411.5.C3S48 1999   635.9'33734'09712   C99-910875-1

The Production Team

Managing Editor:	Thom Shaw
Page Design and Layout:	Melanie Eastley
Illustrations:	Melanie Eastley
Page Composition:	Lu Ziola
Copy Editor:	Lois Hameister
Technical Reviewers:	Shaffeek Ali
	Gordon Heaps
	Gail Rankin
Cover Photographs:	George W. Shewchuk
Front:	Pink Parfait
	Lolita
Back:	Sunset Celebration
	Flower Carpet

All photographs are by the author unless otherwise noted.

My interest in roses stretches over 35 years. The first two or three years of trying to grow roses were abysmal failures, in spite of following the advice given in many publications, and the instructions on packaged roses.

My search for a practical method of wintering tender roses was a long one. I visited many private gardens, as well as the research stations at Beaverlodge, Lacombe, Brooks, Morden, and Ottawa. However, the real breakthrough came when I heard the CBC Winnipeg "Prairie Gardener", Stan Westaway, describe what Percy Wright had been doing for some twenty odd years in the development of hardy roses. Robert Simonet of Edmonton had been doing similar work. The research done at Morden has, perhaps, attained the most success to date. In due time, no doubt, we will have some worthy, hardy Hybrid Tea type roses from these sources.

However, there is sufficient proof that even tender roses can be grown successfully in the harshest agricultural areas of Canada. There is no longer any mystery to growing roses on the plains and prairies. **They are easy to grow, provided they are pampered a little at the correct times.** Inspired by the successful method I found twenty years ago, I have increased the size of my rose beds to include over 350 Hybrid Tea, Grandiflora, Floribunda, Polyantha, and Miniature roses.

It is always a thrill when you discover the first bloom on your new rose bush. It is an even greater thrill when the same bush does well the following year and for several years thereafter. I promise you a beautiful rose garden, provided you follow the advice given in this book. When my suggestions help people grow roses more successfully, I realize my 35 years of work have not been in vain.

From lack of knowledge, many gardeners treat tender roses as annuals, not bothering to protect them over winter, and simply replacing them with new bushes each year. Many other gardeners become discouraged and give up growing roses altogether. This book is written especially for them.

George W. Shewchuk

George W. Shewchuk

Acknowledgments

The University of Alberta Faculty of Extension acknowledges the special contributions made to *Roses: A Gardener's Guide for the Plains and Prairies*, by their technical reviewers: Shaffeek Ali, Gordon Heaps, and Gail Rankin. Their thorough analysis of the work and very detailed recommendations added a new depth and breadth to the publication.

In addition, a special thank you is extended to Scott Reid and Mike Dolinski of Alberta Agriculture, Food and Rural Development, Chris Saunders of the City of Edmonton, and Janet Thornton of the Government of Canada.

Contents

Contents

Chapter 1. History

Chapter 2. How to Use Roses

Chapter 3. Growing Roses

Chapter 4. Selected Roses

Chapter 5. Resource Materials

Chapter One
History

The rose has been called the "Queen of Flowers". For at least 2000 years, it has enjoyed a universal appeal unequalled by any other flower. Since the beginning of recorded history, roses have been symbolic of romance and love and have been present for all types of special occasions.

Sean McCann, a prominent Irish rose grower in Dublin, says, "The rose is still the best and cheapest plant on the market." Even at twice the price, I certainly agree. Another avid rose grower in the United States, Florence Coates, says, "There's always room for beauty – room for another rose." Roses certainly improve the quality of life.

Why Grow Roses?

It is no wonder the rose is such a popular flower. For variety of color, fragrance, and continuity of bloom, no other flower compares with the rose. You can count on a generous supply of blooms from early June throughout summer, until the hard frost nips them in October or November. Few other ornamental plants grow under so many different climatic and soil conditions. Unlike many biennials, perennials, and woody ornamentals, you don't have to wait years for results because roses bloom the first year they are planted. Many people do not consider their gardens complete without roses.

Roses are available in a variety of sizes, from the tiny 6-inch (15 cm) Miniatures up to some of the tall, 6-foot (2 m) Grandifloras, Hybrid Teas, Shrub roses, and climbers which can grow to 12 feet (over 3 m). Roses can be grown as permanent clumps in a flower bed or against a board fence or stone wall. Where space is limited, roses can be grown in a border, along a path, under a picture window, or in groups along a foundation. They can be grown in containers on a balcony or patio, and the Miniatures can be grown indoors or out.

However, to successfully grow roses on the plains and prairies, you must routinely apply a few fundamental procedures. At first, these procedures may seem demanding, even overwhelming, but with a bit of practice, they can be accomplished with relative ease. The author's 350 roses receive an average of about three hours of maintenance each week throughout the growing season. That is not a big sacrifice for the splendor of a beautiful rose garden.

What Roses Tell You

Here are some of the most widely accepted meanings for the different rose colors, blooms, and arrangements:

Red roses: "I love you." They also stand for respect and courage.

White roses: "You are heavenly;" also purity, reverence, and innocence.

Red and white together: Unity.

Pink: Grace and/or gentility.

Deep pink: Gratitude and appreciation.

Yellow: Joy or gladness. It can also say, "Try to care."

Coral or orange: Enthusiasm or desire.

Deep burgundy: Beauty.

Red and yellow blends: Happy and jovial feelings.

Pale colors: Convey sociability and friendship.

Rose buds: Symbolize beauty and/or youth.

White rose buds: Girlhood, "Too young to love."

Wilted white roses: Fleeting beauty; you made no impression.

Single rose: Simplicity.

Single rose in full bloom: "I love you," or "I still love you."

Bouquet of roses in full bloom: Gratitude.

Hybrid tea roses: "I'll remember you always."

Sweetheart roses: "Sweetheart."

Fully open rose placed over two buds: Secrecy.

Two roses tied together to form a single stem: Engagement; a coming marriage.

Red roses say "I love you."

Coral or orange roses communicate enthusiasm or desire.

White roses indicate purity, reverence, and innocence

Yellow roses stand for joy or gladness.

Pink roses stand for grace and/or gentility

Pale colors convey sociability and friendship

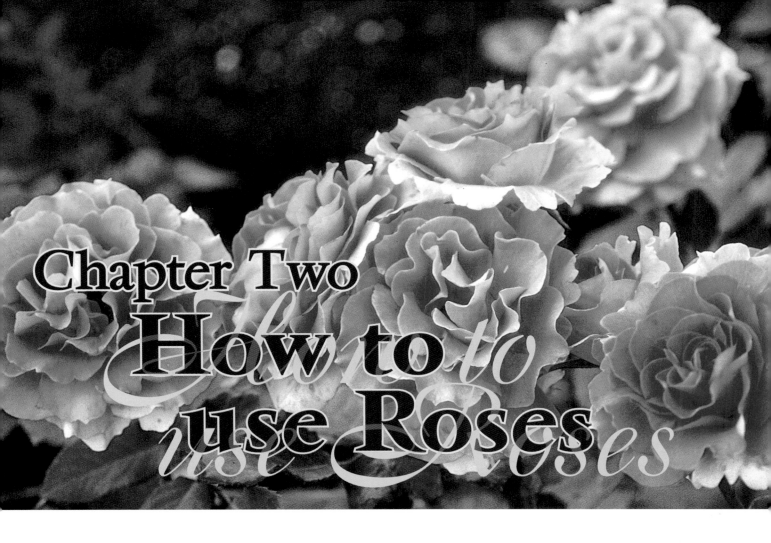

Chapter Two
How to use Roses

Roses in the Landscape

Roses can be used for landscaping in a number of ways. How they are used is determined by their class, hardiness, height and color, and the ability of certain classes to flower continuously. First determine what you want the roses to do in the landscape, and then select the appropriate variety. A few ways roses can be used and what they will do for the landscape are outlined below.

Rose Beds

One popular way of growing roses is in a totally filled bed. Roses in a bed can be more durable, more beautiful, and cheaper substitutes for the once favored annual bedding plants. Floribundas, Grandifloras, and Hybrid Teas make a spectacular show in a single bed, especially when one variety or color is used. This is ideal if you have a large garden area where several beds can be made. If you have a small garden and wish to grow many cultivars, you must sacrifice the masses of color and get to know many cultivars

intimately. One way to partially get around this is to group roses of similar color together, but you must know your rose cultivars well to do this successfully.

Miniature roses mix well with many annuals in flower beds. For bloom production, they are hard to beat. They bloom from early spring until frost.

Massed plantings in beds can create interesting and beautiful pockets in landscape and foundation plantings. They are equally effective when grown in some out-of-the-way garden location to serve as a source of cut flowers.

Hedge patterns

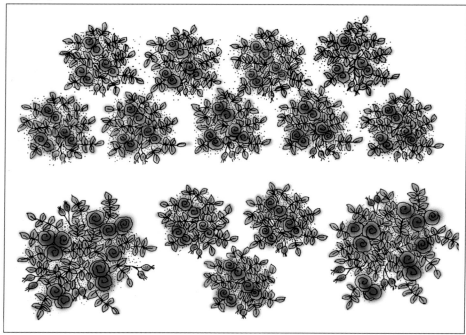

Hedges

Certain rose cultivars are perfect when a natural, free growing type of hedge is required. Roses are not suitable for a tall, narrow hedge or one that is squared off. They may be planted in one or more rows as desired, using one cultivar or a mixture of cultivars. The choice of cultivar or variety for a hedge depends to a large extent on how much time you have. If you wish to have a beautiful, colorful hedge, plant remontant (continuous flowering) Floribunda or Shrub roses (see Chapter 4). However, when Floribundas are chosen, you must use the winter protection methods recommended in this book. Interesting groupings can be used in a two row hedge. Two possible ideas are shown above.

Roses in a perennial border

Ground Cover

In the last few years, many low-growing hardy cultivars have been developed which serve very well as ground covers. Some are so aggressive that no other low-growing plant is able to invade the occupied area. While serving as ground covers, they also produce a profusion of blooms.

Cultivars suitable for ground covers include:
- Bonica
- Carefree Delight
- Charles Albanel
- Flower Carpet
- Pavement Roses
- Ralph's Creeper
- Royal Edward
- The Fairy
- Topaz Jewel
- Charles Albanel, Royal Edward and Topaz Jewel (these are considered the hardiest).

Perennial Border

A perennial border can be made of roses alone or in combination with other herbaceous plants. Roses offer a variety of heights and colors to make many interesting possibilities. Grouping of three to five bushes of a variety give spectacular results.

Where a longer continuity of bloom is desirable, roses may be successfully substituted for peonies and delphiniums. This also applies to other commonly used perennial flowers.

Roses in a mixed planting

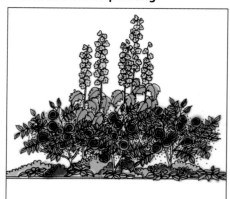

Climbers

Large container (raised bed)

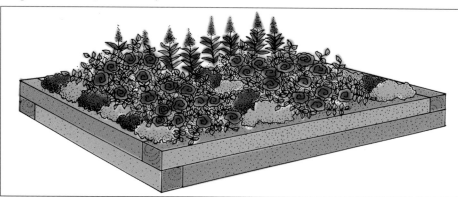

Foundation Planting

Shrub roses, which are very hardy and easy to grow and unlike the more tender roses require no special winter protection, are commonly used in landscaping and foundation plantings. However, with improved wintering techniques, some very commendable foundation plantings using Hybrid Teas, Grandifloras, and Floribundas can be achieved.

Decorating and Covering Arbors, Trellises, Walks, and Fences

Climbing roses are now available that can be used to enhance the appearance of any wall, fence, trellis, or arbor. There are varieties hardy for the northern areas which require little or no winter protection, and for those who are willing to provide winter protection, there is a long list to choose from. See Chapter 4.

Containers

Roses are ideal for planters, boxes, pots, and hanging baskets. However, container size must be carefully matched to the rose's growth or habit to achieve optimum results.

Container grown roses can add interesting accent points when placed strategically about the garden or patio.

Cultivars adapted to container growing are shown in the table below.. For those living in town houses and condominiums with only a balcony, it is the only way to grow roses outdoors. The section Growing Roses In Containers provides specific details on the growth needs of container grown roses.

Potted miniatures

Roses Suitable for Container Growing

Hybrid Tea	Floribundas	Miniatures (hanging basket)	Miniatures	Polyanthas
Alpine Sunset (apricot blend)	Brass Band (apricot blend)	Candy Lane (pink blend)	Jean Kenneally (apricot blend)	China Doll (medium pink)
Double Delight (red & creamy white)	Cherish (orange pink)	Jeanne Lajoie (medium pink)	Minnie Pearl (pink blend)	Orange Morsdag (orange blend)
Granada (scarlet & yellow)	Class Act (white)	Little Girl (orange pink)	Pacesetter (white)	Perle d'Or (yellow blend)
Honor (white)	Marlena (medium red)	Earthquake (red blend)	Pierrine (orange pink)	The Fairy (light pink)
Lady Diana (light pink)	Pleasure (medium pink)	Over The Rainbow (red blend)	Rise 'n' Shine (medium yellow)	Lullaby (white)
Secret (pink blend)	Sexy Rexy (medium pink)	Phyllis Bide (yellow blend)	Starina (orange red)	Verdun (medium red)

Showing Roses

Types of Display or Staging

Roses can be exhibited in many ways. Here are a few representative classes selected from various show schedules:

- Single stem, one bloom
- Hybrid Tea – fully open (fully blown)
- Vase of roses
- Collection of five Hybrid Teas
- Collection of different types of roses
- Bowl – single specimen
- Bowl – arrangement
- English Box – six specimen bloom
- Rose arrangement
- Rose bouquet
- Corsage and boutonniere
- Cycle of bloom
- Potted Miniature rose
- Miniature English Box
- Miniature rose – one bloom
- Miniature rose – one spray
- Grandiflora rose – one spray – one bloom (could be divided to accommodate various colors)
- Floribunda rose – one spray – one bloom (could be divided to accommodate various colors)

This is not a definitive list but merely indicates some of the very many classes possible. The descriptions that follow are intended to illustrate some of the important considerations in the various classes. Check the show regulations, ask questions of organizers, and see Resource Materials section for more information.

Single Stem, One Bloom

This class is generally used for Hybrid Teas but may be used for Floribundas, Grandifloras, and Miniatures.

Unless the single specimen class at the show calls for fully open blooms, double bloom roses look best when they are one-half to three-quarters open; single and semi-double blooms look best when fully open.

Full bloom is the stage when all

Single stem, one bloom

petals are symmetrically unfurled and arranged within a circular outline. Buds are not suitable as rose show specimens. A bud is considered to be a bud up to the stage of development where it is beginning to show full color, with only one or two petals commencing to unfurl above an opening calyx.

One bloom specimens should have stems to complement the bloom. In most cases, it is a stem with at least two sets of five or more leaflets. The exhibitor should not be overly concerned if the stem does not come up to this rigid specification, as long as the foliage is pleasing to the eye and has proper balance and proportion.

Single specimen rose exhibits are shown with no side buds. These should be removed when very small so that it does not show any signs of removal or scars. It is best done about twenty days before the show.

A stem-on-stem is a bloom which has a portion of the primary stem from which a bloom had been removed.

Some people do this to get a longer stem for better looking balance and proportion. The older portion of such a stem is generally hidden in a vase at shows to conceal it from judges and rosarians. Most of the time, when there are any doubts, the specimen is lifted out of the vase for examination.

Hybrid Tea — Fully Open

In the many-petalled roses, the Fully Open phase occurs on a bloom that is getting old and almost ready to shed its petals. It is a condition of the bloom in which all the petals have uncurled as far as possible. Those with 25 to 40 petals will have the center and stamens visible. Roses with more petals will have all their petals unfurled and not expose the stamens.

Stem-on-stem

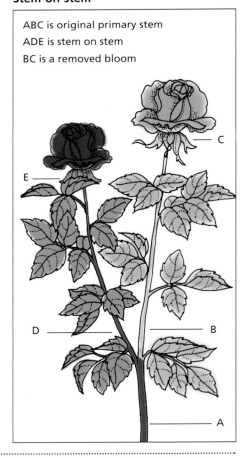

ABC is original primary stem
ADE is stem on stem
BC is a removed bloom

Hybrid tea – fully open

Bowl – single specimen

Bowl – arrangement

There are varieties of Hybrid Tea roses that have only a few (5 to 20) petals. When their buds open up, they immediately become fully open (the center is clearly visible). These are not intended for this class. The Fully Open class is intended for the many-petalled varieties. They are allowed to open as far as possible and still look attractive.

Vase of Roses

This class calls for either three to five or more long-stemmed roses in a vase. Show rules may call for one color only, harmonious colors, or different colors. Make sure you use a regulation container (check the show rules). Remove lower thorns and leaves—those which may be inside the container.

Collection of Five Hybrid Teas

Usually five different cultivars are used and exhibited in individual containers. Try to have blooms of uniform size with stems the same length.

Collection of Different Types of Roses

This class is to show the different types of roses available: for example, Hybrid Tea, Grandiflora, Floribunda, Polyantha, and Miniature.

Bowl — Single Specimen

A fully open bloom is floated on one or two rose leaves in about 1 inch (2.5 cm) of water in a bowl (large blooms are best for this). The stem is cut very short so that the bloom rests flat on the leaf on top of the water.

English Box

These boxes are specially built to facilitate exhibiting 6, 9, 12, 15, 18, or 24 short-stemmed roses. The larger blossoms are placed in the back tubes. The most popular in the United States and Canada is the box of six. No foliage is required. This type of exhibit is popular with gardeners who do not have the well-foliaged, long-stemmed, "regal" type roses. The flower size should be uniform, and the degree of openness is important — preferably two-thirds to three-quarters open. The color of each flower should complement the others in the box if possible. A regular size box for six blooms is 7½ × 14½ inches (19 × 37 cm), and 1 inch (2.5 cm) higher at one end than the other.

Bowl — Arrangement

Specimens for this class require medium length stems. Each bloom in this bowl arrangement must be clear of its neighbor. Do not allow blooms to touch each other and yet avoid having large gaps between them.

English box

Rose arrangement

Mini English box

Cycle of bloom

Rose Arrangement

This class is generally left to the exhibitor's imagination, ingenuity, and good taste. Show rules will give specifics as to foliage permitted and the occasion for which it is intended.

Corsage

Rose Bouquet

A rose bouquet consists of anywhere from 6 to 12 long-stemmed roses of a single color, or a pleasing, harmonious combination of colors. The stems must be of equal length. There is no special arrangement required for this exhibit.

Corsage and Boutonniere

Small Hybrid Tea type blossoms are excellent for corsages and boutonnieres. The cultivar Faberge continues to win many awards in this class. The flowers are long-lasting, beautifully sculptured, slightly fragrant, and excellent in form, both in the bud and fully open stages. Also very good for the petite corsage is the Polyantha, light pink colored rose, Cecile Brunner. For a boutonniere, a rose just starting to open, with sepals down, all color showing, and petals still unfurling is ideal in this class.

Cycle of Bloom

The cycle of bloom should show three stages of bloom of the same cultivar of a Hybrid Tea type; one bud, one show form bloom, and one full bloom. The bud should have the color just beginning to show, sepals down, and petals just starting to unfurl. The show form bloom should be one-half to three-quarters open depending on the number of petals in the bloom (the more petals, the more open it should be). The fully blown bloom must show stamens.

Potted Miniature Rose

The pot for the Miniature rose should not exceed 9 inches (23 cm). Check the rules and prize schedule closely as this could vary from show to show. There may be a class for a potted, Miniature standard rose as well.

Miniature English Box

In all respects this class is the same as the regular English Box except for size. The same rules apply as to uniformity of size, degree of openness, color match, and harmony. The box should measure 4 × 7 inches (10 × 18 cm).

Miniature Rose — One Bloom

Miniature roses reflect the form, color, substance, and size of all the types of the larger Hybrid Teas. In form they have a greater variation and are judged on their own individual merits. The point scoring system is the same as for the Hybrid Teas.

Spray of Floribunda roses

Miniature Rose — One Spray

The Miniature spray is judged on the same basis as set for judging Floribunda roses.

Grandiflora Rose — One Spray

The objective in a Grandiflora spray is to create a mass display of blooms at the same stage of development. All things being equal, a cultivar showing mass blooming should win over one showing various stages of bloom. When the first bud is removed, most Grandifloras produce blooms in mass effect. This is more the accepted ideal, with flower form also getting important consideration. The spray should show two or more blooms.

Floribunda Rose — One Spray

Floribundas are judged on the basis of showing the various stages of development. Ideally, the Floribunda inflorescence should show all stages of development:
* green buds
* beginning to unfurl
* one-third open
* one-half open
* three-quarters open
* fully open.

Some cultivars, because of their characteristics, open to the same stage of development at the same time, usually full blown. Other cultivars exhibit two stages, bud and full blown. For a maximum score, the number of mature flowers should be more in evidence than the buds and less developed florets. The overall appearance of the inflorescence, rather than the form of each individual bloom, is of prime importance.

Differences in Canadian and American Judging Guidelines

The American and Canadian Judging and Point Systems are essentially the same even though there are minor differences in the awarding of points. The American Rose Society uses small letters to denote color, for example, rb for red blend. The Canadian Rose Society uses capital letters, RB. I prefer to use the small letters. If you write Pascali W HT and Pascali w HT, or Oriana RB HT and Oriana rb HT, it becomes apparent which is easier to interpret.

Judge's Point System – American Rose Society Guidelines for Hybrid Teas	
Form	25 points
Color	20 points
Substance	15 points
Stem and foliage	20 points
Balance and proportion	10 points
Size	10 points
Total	**100 points**

Judge's Point System – Canadian Rose Society Guidelines for Hybrid Teas	
Form	25 points
Color	25 points
Substance	20 points
Stem, foliage, & balance	20 points
Size	10 points
Total	**100 points**

Detailed Judging Information

To give detailed information for judging Grandiflora, Floribunda, Polyantha, Miniature, Shrub, Climber, Fragrant, Old Garden roses, Collections, English Box, bowls, rose in a bowl, vase, bouquet, and other important points requires a lengthy script which may be enough for a sizeable manual.

For those who want a lot of detail and to become judges, it is best to obtain a *Guide for Judging Roses* from the Canadian Rose Society and the American Rose Society. Addresses for these societies are given at the back of this book under Useful Reference Books.

This scoring system allocates values to the various rose attributes. It is mainly used when tight decisions have to be made. The point system is also used to average a score when more than one judge is evaluating an exhibit.

An exhibitor must be aware that the point system is not used by the judge in a formal way for every rose judged. That would take hours to complete. However, it gives a novice judge an idea of the relative values of the various components. The point scoring system also assists rose exhibitors in meeting the criteria.

Form

This is the most valuable attribute in an exhibition rose. Generally, the most perfect phase of beauty is when a rose is one-half to three-quarters open. It must be symmetrical, with a circular outline. It must have a sufficient number of petals, be gracefully shaped, and appear to be high centered. Rose cultivars with fewer petals are in the most perfect phase when one-half to two-thirds open and should have at least 3 to 4 rows of petals unfurling.

Blooms with a larger number of petals than average should be two-thirds to three-quarters open, and have at least 4 to 5 rows of petals unfurling.

The bud stage of growth continues to the point where the sepals are down, petals just beginning to unfurl, and the configuration of the center is not evident. A bud is not a bloom and cannot be considered for any award for a bloom.

The decorative type Hybrid Teas vary somewhat from the standard Hybrid Teas in that they may not have a well-defined high and pointed center. It may be ruffled and cupped, and can have a low, sunken, rather than pointed, center. Otherwise they have identical judging standards.

Single Hybrid Tea roses have from 5 to 12 petals. They are judged to be at perfection when fully opened. They may be shown as one bloom or as a spray.

Color

Color is composed of hue, chroma, and brightness. Hue is the factor that gives visual impact to the eye and distinguishes one color from another. Chroma is the purity and intensity of the hue. Brightness is the clarity of the hue (free of cloudiness).

The Canadian Rose Society Guidelines list the following color classes (the small letters following the color indicate the American Rose Society abbreviation for the color often used in rose literature. The Canadian Rose Society has these capitalized):

- White or near white – w
- Light yellow – ly
- Medium yellow – my
- Deep yellow – dy
- Yellow blend – yb
- Apricot – a
- Apricot blend – ab
- Orange – o
- Orange blend – ob
- Orange pink – op
- Orange red – or
- Light pink – lp
- Medium pink – mp
- Deep pink – dp
- Pink blend – pb
- Medium red – mr
- Dark red – dr
- Red blend – rb
- Mauve – m
- Mauve blend – mb
- Russet – r

There are also the bi-colors. These roses have one color when viewed from the top, but show a different color on the reverse side of the petal. Good examples of this are:

- Oriana – red with a white reverse. Red color predominates; it is therefore marked rb.
- Miss Canada – pink with a silvery-white reverse. Pink color predominates; therefore it is marked pb.

Stem, Foliage, Balance, and Proportion

The stem should be straight, the proper length, not too coarse or too thin, and with typical thorns. Too long a stem makes the specimen lanky and out of proportion to the size of the flower. Sparse foliage makes the specimen appear armless and ill. The foliage should be undamaged, clean, well groomed, of sufficient number, and of proper size. A stem-on-stem specimen is disqualified.

Disbudding should be done at an early stage so that the resulting scar will be as small as possible and not too noticeable.

A stem with two (three leaflet) leaves above three (5, 7, or 9 leaflet) leaves generally presents a complete specimen.

The balance and proportion of a rose refers to the overall pleasing appearance of the specimen. This is judged by how

Full blown with stamens showing

Three-quarters open

Various stages of bloom

Fully open

One-third to one-half open

the bloom relates to the stem and foliage, and how the bloom, stem, and foliage complement each other (one being not too large or too small for the other).

Substance

Substance is rated as the keeping quality of the rose. It is constituted by texture, crispness, firmness, thickness, and toughness of the petals. Loss of substance is first evident by a faint browning and discoloring of the edges of the outer petals. Quite often the stamens indicate the substance in the petals. A rose with good substance will have nicely colored stamens that stand up well and are not discolored. (This applies to single and semi-double roses.)

Size

This actually refers to the average size of the bloom. All other things being equal, normal size can become the determining factor in placing one specimen over another. A bloom that is clearly undersized or oversized will receive a small penalty.

Danish Judging System

This is an alternative to the regular and familiar system where exhibits are awarded only for the first, second, and third placings in a class, no matter how many good exhibits there are. The Danish System recognizes all worthy exhibits. It also recognizes that it is very rare to find a worthless exhibit. Our agricultural departments have long ago recognized the value of this system and adopted it for the Future Farmers of America and 4-H clubs.

We all know that in many cases good and worthy exhibits get no award and recognition. This is very discouraging to exhibitors and quite often the public. With the Danish Judging System all worthy exhibits are given some recognition and awards are given on a group or point basis.

The exhibits are placed by the judge into four groups – A, B, C, and D

according to their general quality. In group A the exhibits may receive 10, 9, or 8 points or fractions thereof (e.g., 8.5, 8.7, 9.1, 9.2). A full 10 points is very seldom used. That would denote perfection. The general belief is that there is nothing that is perfect; there is always room for improvement. Exhibitors in this group receive a first prize ribbon with a corresponding number of points. In Group B, the exhibits may receive 7 and 6 points, and a second place ribbon (exhibits are of a slightly lower quality); Group C receives 5 and 4 points and a third place ribbon; Group D receives 3, 2, and 1 points and a fourth place ribbon.

Prize money, if there is any, is given out according to the group award or points earned. For example, the show recorder adds the points earned by all the exhibitors. Suppose this adds up to 10,000 points. If the Society has only $300 available for awards, the $300 is divided by 10,000 which equals 3 cents per point. If an exhibitor earned 100 points, the award is 100 times 3 cents or $3. This is simple to do and should not present any mathematical problem. If there are insufficient funds for monetary awards, most exhibitors are happy to receive a ribbon in recognition of their efforts.

The Danish System is considered by many to be the fairest ever devised. The only drawback is that it requires a little more studying by the judge and requires a greater number of ribbons.

This system is gaining popularity where show societies are concerned with the declining number of exhibitors, exhibits, and viewers.

Special Advice

Hints On Showing Roses

Grandifloras, Floribundas, Polyanthas, and Climbers are exhibited as clusters or trusses of flowers on a single stem, unless the class in the prize list calls for one bloom, one stem. Buds are

permitted in the cluster. The overall form of the spray can take the shape of a circle, oval, or any other geometric form pleasing to the eye. From the side, the spray can take on a flat appearance, with all the florets on the same level, or a domed appearance. To present a good appearance, spent blooms and unwanted growth may be removed if it is done without impairing the exhibit.

All roses must be named correctly. Where variety name is stressed, judges may disqualify blooms that are without labels or are incorrectly named. Rose shows enable gardeners to select cultivars to try in their own garden.

Crooked stems can be straightened by tying the stem to a stake in at least three different places about two weeks before the show. The leaves will take their normal position to the sun in that time.

For show purposes, it is essential that the rose be clean and free of chemical

Staking roses

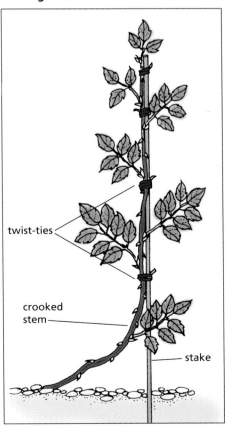

twist-ties

crooked stem

stake

Protecting blooms from weather

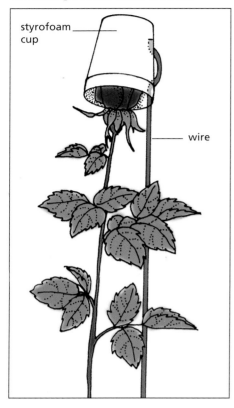

styrofoam cup

wire

residue, dust, disease, and insects. Foliage may be cleaned by wiping it with a moist, soft flannel cloth. Other foreign material on the bloom can be removed with a camel's hair brush.

To have the rose specimen show some freshness, it is necessary to cut it as close to show time as possible. Cutting and preserving roses is important. Refer to the sections on Basic Pruning, and Keeping Cut Flowers, for additional information.

Occasionally, you may have a bloom that is opening in a lopsided manner. It can be manipulated into proper shape by careful use of a soft camel's hair brush. Begin by carefully manipulating the brush inside the outer row, and then into the next row of petals as required. To do this effectively, practice on several blooms not intended for showing. Before using the brush, try blowing into the bloom. The warm air blast may be all that is necessary to open it up. The camel's hair brush can also be used to open up a bloom that may be too tight for exhibition.

Tips of petals that have been bruised or torn may be skilfully sheared away with sharp manicure scissors. A damaged leaf can similarly be manicured. Done with care, the damaged part will hardly be noticeable.

A single, prized bloom can be protected from rain or hot sun by placing a styrofoam cup over it. Do not let the cup touch the bloom. The cup is adjusted to the proper height by sticking the wire end into the ground. A twist-tie wrapped around the rose cane and wire will keep the cup from vibrating and rubbing the bloom during a wind storm.

Waxing or oiling of foliage does not improve the appearance. Rose foliage is best when exhibited in its natural healthy state. Whether foliage is glossy or matte-textured depends on the variety.

Rose Bloom Faults

The following are common faults that rose exhibitors must avoid:
- Too many or too few petals result in a form not typical for the cultivar.
- Petals are not regularly arranged to form a circular outline when viewed from the top and the bloom lacks symmetry.
- A split or confused center is a faulty arrangement of petals in the center of the bloom, giving the appearance of a double center. A prominent split is much more serious than one that is just beginning to show.
- Dwarfed and distorted blooms and buds caused by mildew, excess rain, and insects are also faulted.

Keeping Cut Flowers

The proper way of cutting and handling roses can add days of life to your display flowers.

Use a very sharp knife—the cleaner the cut, the better the stem is able take up water. Most florists prefer a slant cut because it creates a greater area for water absorption. Dull cutting instruments have a tendency to crush the stem end. This reduces water uptake.

Confused center

Place your cut roses in a bucket or other container as they are cut. Use a bucket that has been cleaned thoroughly. Any bacteria or fungi in the container can grow rapidly and soon kill your flowers. Some people use aspirin, copper pennies, sugar, and soft drinks in the flower vases. These may be harmful if used without a bactericide or fungicide. They stimulate the growth of bacteria and fungi that clog the water conducting tissue in the stem. It is better to invest your time and money in a good floral preservative such as Petal Life, Rose Life, Bloom Life, or Floralife. It is difficult to keep bacteria and fungi out of water without a preservative. Changing the water every day helps, but it will not eliminate microbial growth. De-ionized or boiled water is much better for cut flowers than tap water. Cut plants take in several times the amount of de-ionized or boiled water than tap water.

The best time to cut roses is when the temperature is cool – in the evening or early morning. Take your bucket with warm water around 104°F (40°C), with preservative, to the garden where you are cutting. Place the cut flowers into this solution immediately. Any delay will cause air to enter the water-conducting tissue in the cut end. This will prevent water from being taken up by the plant. Re-cutting under water will guarantee that no air is taken in. Hold the roses in a warm solution for 1 to 2 hours. This helps the flowers to quickly absorb water. Following this, place them in cool, "preservative spiked", de-ionized water in a cool dark place for 4 to 8 hours. This is called "conditioning".

Following the conditioning, roses may be refrigerated at around 35°F (1 to 2°C), or they may be displayed or arranged. Again, take the same precautions by using clean vases, or bowls, de-ionized water, a preservative, and a fresh cut on each stem. The foliage below the water level should be stripped. Leaves under water start decaying very rapidly. This procedure will double the life of cut roses, so it is well worth the effort. Cut flower and foliage deterioration is ten times faster at 70°F (20°C) than at 32°F (0°C).

Cutting roses at the proper stage of maturity is important. If cut when buds are too tight, they will never open. If left too long, they will be past their prime. A good time to cut them is when two or three outer petals are starting to unfold. To keep roses from opening too fast, wrap a piece of paper loosely around the bloom, hold in place with tape, and keep refrigerated at around 35°F (1 to 2°C).

Do not keep fruit in a refrigerator used for storing roses. The ethene (also ethylene) gas given off by ripening fruit damages roses.

Restoring Wilted Roses

Wilted cut roses can be revived and made to look quite presentable. Immerse the roses, leaves and all, in 104°F (40°C) water in a bathtub. Cut 1 inch (2.5 cm) off their stem ends under water. Make sure the stems and necks are straightened or they will come out firm but bent. One hour under water will straighten them out and make them look fresh again.

Transporting Roses

Transporting roses can present serious problems. Cut roses should not be exposed to sun, wind, heat, or extreme cold. Roses can be taken for a considerable distance in one of several ways:

- Wrap each rose separately in a soft, florist waxed paper and lay them in a box with a roll of newspaper for a neck pillow. Place plastic bags of ice at the base of stems and fasten securely.
- Transport rose specimens long distances in long individual tubes with some water in the base.
- Wrap each rose separately as described previously and place in a partially filled pail of iced water.

Other Uses

Arrangements

Remember the elegance of a banquet, wedding, or awards dinner when there is a large arrangement of roses on a table. Very few flowers enhance the occasion more than an arrangement of roses.

Enhanced Displays

Homes, gardens, and some commercial businesses are greatly enhanced, appear happier, and present a peaceful, lived-in look, where flowers, especially roses, are artfully and strategically placed for people to view and admire. Astute business people know this attracts people and business.

Bouquet

A bouquet is simply a number of long-stemmed roses, in no special arrangement, with their stems tied together. A dozen roses of a single color make a very generous and impressive bouquet.

There are few things as heart-warming as receiving a bouquet of roses from a loved one.

Boutonniere or Corsage

Have you ever noticed how proudly a rose corsage is worn? A corsage should be worn with flowers pointing upward, and if there is a ribbon or bow, it should be at the base of the corsage.

Single Cut Flower

A single rose in a suitable container (a crystal vase) epitomizes true, simple natural beauty. A single, simple rose makes a clear statement of admiration. Its unique sweet fragrance and simple beauty is unsurpassed by any other flower.

Thank You, Happy Birthday, Happy Anniversary, I Love You, Retirement, and Congratulations can all be said eloquently with roses. If you are looking for a unique way to say something appropriate on any special occasion, say it with roses. What nicer way is there to be remembered than with roses!

Roses As House Plants

Roses make interesting and beautiful plants when grown in a bright, sunny window or under artificial lights. When you grow roses in the home, humidity problems are usually encountered during the winter months. To help relieve this problem, the "Gravel Tray" technique may be used. A shallow tray is filled with marble-sized pebbles about 1¼ inches (3 cm) deep. Pour water into the tray until it rises to within ½ inch (1 cm) of the top of the pebbles. Place the potted roses on top of the pebbles. As the water in the bottom of the tray evaporates, it provides some of the humidity necessary for the plants.

The most suitable roses for house plants are those commonly used as Mother's Day gifts and Miniatures. Many types of potted roses are commonly seen on the market around Mother's Day.

Further information on this subject can be found under the section, Growing Under Artificial Lights.

Dried Rose Blooms

Drying rose blooms is quite a popular hobby. If you are interested, obtain a good manual from a hobby shop on how to preserve flowers. Rose shows often have beautiful exhibits of dried Miniature roses. This is the perfect place to gain information on the processes and arrangements.

Potpourri

Dried fragrant rose petals are spiced and kept in decorative jars or small pillows used to scent a room, chest of drawers, or clothes closets.

Perfume Crafting

Rosewater, cologne, and fragrant oil can be made from rose petals.

Here is a simple method for creating rosewater:

½ cup water

1 quart rose petals

Place petals and water in a saucepan. Bring to a boil and let simmer for 15 minutes covered and another 5 minutes uncovered. Strain and funnel into your chosen small bottle.

Rose Hip Vitamin Source

Rose hips, especially the large red ripe ones, are rich in Vitamin C and other elements known for centuries for their emotionally soothing properties. A single cup of pared rose hips may contain as much Vitamin C as 10 to 12 dozen oranges.

Because of a limited commercial supply, it is difficult to find rose hips in our food stores. The aboriginal people of Saskatchewan have found a market in Japan for all the Prairie Wild Rose hips they are able to gather. In Japan the valuable Vitamin C is extracted and sold to health food stores.

CAUTION: Garden grown roses are usually sprayed or dusted with toxic chemicals to protect them from disease and insect damage. Roses grown with the support of pesticides must **not** be used for any edible purpose! No one should risk ingesting potentially hazardous chemicals. If your roses are grown without the use of insecticides and fungicides, experiment with the various culinary uses that follow.

Rose Hip Jam and Jelly

Anyone who has eaten rose hip jam will want to get more or make some of their own. It is delicious with a wonderful, delicate flavor of its own. Libraries, bookstores, and home canning experts can help you find successful recipes for making rose hip jam and jelly. Here is a simple recipe for jelly:

6 cups rose hips

½ bottle liquid pectin

2 cups water

4 cups super fine sugar

Pare the bud ends of the rose hips, and coarsely grind them. Heat pulp and water in a 3 to 4 quart saucepan over low heat. Bring to a simmer for one hour or until the pulp is very tender. Strain through a cheesecloth or jelly bag into a sufficiently large bowl. Clean the pot and add 3 cups of juice and 4 cups of sugar. Bring to a boil, stirring constantly, and then add the fruit pectin. Return to a boil for another four minutes and remove from the heat. Skim the surface, pour into sterilized jelly jars, and seal.

Rose Wine

Wine making is a very specialized and sophisticated process. It is best to obtain a book focusing on home wine making to get explicit instructions on making rose wine, as well as wine from many other fruits and berries. By following the recommended procedures, you can produce a very fine wine from both rose hips and petals.

Rose Liqueur

A liqueur with a bouquet and taste that is soft and flowery can be easily made with these simple ingredients:

40 rose petals

1¼ cups water

1½ cups sugar

2 cups vodka

Mix rose petals and ½ cup of sugar thoroughly. Add some of the vodka and beat for a few minutes. Pour this mixture, plus the rest of the vodka, into a jar with a tightly sealed lid. Shake well. Let stand for ten days but shake well a few times to help mix the ingredients. Next, dissolve 1 cup of sugar in 1¼ cups of boiling water and let cool completely. Add to the contents in the jar, seal again, and shake well. Let stand for one week. Then strain through a colander and cheesecloth into a jar. Seal tightly and store in a cool, dark place for three months.

Rose Petal Tea

Tea made from fragrant rose petals or rose hips is a delicacy. A small handful of fresh fragrant rose petals in an average tea pot (4 to 5 cups) makes a unique and delicious tea. Rose petals can also be dried and kept for future use in an air-tight container. Use about two tablespoons of dried rose flowers per cup, add boiling water and steep for five minutes. Add sugar or honey to taste to help bring out the fragrance.

The best petals are from the native roses growing across the plains and prairies in an area free of possible chemical residue from field crop and roadside spraying for weeds, insects, and diseases. Native wild rose petals have a strong pleasant fragrance.

Chapter Three
Growing Roses

Roses are perennial plants and thus expected to last for several years. Before you even start digging, there are many things to consider. This section is a simple guide for avoiding serious pitfalls.

Planning the Rose Garden

All landscapers advise you to plan before you plant. It is easier to change the plan than to dig and re-plant at a later date. Although roses make up only a small portion of the total home landscape, they should fit and add interest and beauty to the complete plan.

Paper and Pencil Planning

A garden plan is just as important as a house plan. The garden and the home are part of each other and should be thought of as a complete unit. If well planned, a very pleasant living area is created.

In order to properly proportion the areas for plantings, it is necessary to have a plan drawn to scale. If you draw several plans, you can choose and integrate the best aspects of each. Try to involve all the members of the household in determining your basic requirements for the garden – shelter, recreational areas, lawn, vegetables, trees, and shrubs, plus annual and perennial flowers.

Take the following steps when planning your rose garden:
- Consider your budget.
- Choose the size, shape, and location of the rose bed or beds.

Garden plan

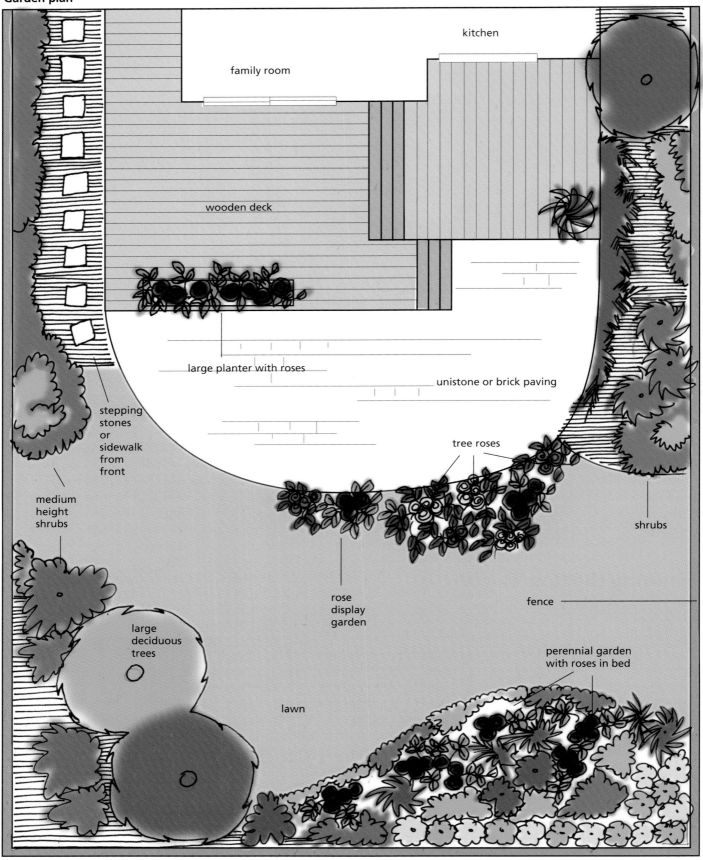

kitchen

family room

wooden deck

large planter with roses

unistone or brick paving

stepping stones or sidewalk from front

medium height shrubs

tree roses

shrubs

rose display garden

fence

large deciduous trees

lawn

perennial garden with roses in bed

Root barrier

- Examine soil conditions, drainage, water, shelter, and other aspects of plant care.
- Select the number of roses of each kind (class), variety, and color needed.
- Choose a rose supplier.
- Plan for the storage of equipment and materials needed to maintain the garden.

This publication gives you specific guidelines for a successful rose garden but cannot cover all aspects of planning a garden. Each garden plan must be geared to the individual needs and wishes of the occupants.

Location and Exposure

Provide protection for the rose beds from most of the strong prevailing winds and storms. A tall, solid board or picket fence makes a good shelter. Tree and hedge shelters provide better protection, but you must be certain that tree roots and shade do not interfere with the rose bed. Roses should be kept away from large trees like birch, spruce, ash, elm, or maple. Also beware of poplars: Northwest, Russian, Griffin, Tower, native Black Poplar, Balm-of-Gilead, and the native White Poplar (Trembling Aspen). These trees have tremendously long and shallow roots that can extend a distance equal to 2½ times their height.

In most gardens it is difficult to locate rose beds a safe distance from large trees on the property. In such cases a barrier between the trees and the rose bed can be installed. This can be achieved by digging a trench 2 feet (60 cm) deep and installing heavy gauge galvanized tin, fibre-glass, or 12 mil polyethylene, standing on edge to the surface level. Overlap pieces 3 to 4 inches (8 to 10 cm)

and caulk the ends. A crack or hole in the barrier is sure to be found by tree roots. Refill the trench and the barrier will not be noticeable. An alternative would be to grow roses in containers in the vicinity of large invasive trees.

Roses cannot be grown in shade; they require sunlight for at least eight hours per day. Less than this will result in weak, spindly, and unproductive rose bushes.

If your roses are exposed to prevailing winds, protect them with a lattice work, board fence, or tree shelter. However, if this is not possible or practical, do not deprive yourself of an abundance of beautiful roses. Plant roses regardless of the risk.

Color In Rose Beds

Many people prefer to grow roses in formal plantings using only one cultivar or color in each bed to give a breathtaking splash of color. Each cultivar has its own bloom cycle and if a bed contains only a single cultivar and color, there will be a flowerless period before another flush of bloom appears. Other gardeners prefer mixed cultivars in each bed to get away from the "barren look" between blooming periods. Another alternative for very color conscious individuals is to group different cultivars and types of roses of similar color. This will give the desired color and a long continuous period of bloom. However, for this system to work, the rose grower must know rose cultivars and types very well.

You can create any color combination you wish, but in small areas and small beds, mixed colors lose their effectiveness. It is best to group three to five bushes of the same cultivar and color together. In larger areas, mixed colors can present a riot of color if that is your wish.

Selecting Roses

If you are inexperienced, selecting roses can be a bewildering experience when you browse through a busy garden center or study a rose catalogue. This chapter is written to help you find and buy the best.

Types of Bush Roses

Roses are available in at least forty-five different classes. The most common rose classes grown on the plains and prairies include:

Hybrid Tea
Floribunda
Grandiflora
Polyantha
Climbing
Ramblers
Miniature
Moss
Shrub
Sweetheart
Standard Tree

Note: The Standard Tree rose is a specimen with one or more grafts on the top of a tall rose cane.

Hybrid Tea Roses

The most popular of all roses are Hybrid Tea roses. These plants grow into bushes from 2 to 5 feet (60 to 150 cm). The popular Hybrid Teas have long pointed buds and high centered blooms with strong, straight stems. They make excellent show roses and are usually the type sold by florists. Most are double-blossomed; they bear anywhere from 20 to 70 velvet-textured petals. A few Hybrid Tea cultivars such as Dainty Bess, White Wings, Safrano, American Flagship, Golden Butterfly, Allegratto, and Innocence have single and semi-double blossoms and from 5 to 20 petals.

The leaves of Hybrid Tea roses are generally dark or medium green. A few cultivars start their new foliage as dark red, then turn to green. Their texture varies from glossy and leathery to dull (matte) in appearance.

Hybrid Tea roses can now be obtained in almost any color or color combination. They are suitable for planting in a bed or in groups in a border to supplement other plantings.

Floribunda Roses

Floribundas first originated from crosses made with Polyanthas and Hybrid Teas in 1922. The flowers of Floribunda bushes come in clusters of single or double bloom on each stem. They are everblooming and present a wonderful display starting in June and ending with the arrival of killing frost in the fall.

Floribundas are generally lower in height than Hybrid Teas but are considered slightly hardier. Each year, more and better Floribundas are developed. Because of the profusion and consistency of bloom, they have become increasingly more popular since the 1940s. They are excellent for use where an abundance of color is desired.

Grandiflora Roses

Grandifloras are hybrids resulting from crosses made between Floribundas and Hybrid Tea roses in 1955. This crossing combined the good qualities of the free flowering Floribundas with the magnificent long-stemmed Hybrid Teas. They grow to about the same height as Hybrid Teas. The flowers come in clusters that are only slightly smaller than the Hybrid Teas. The stems are longer than those of the Floribundas. The buds and flowers resemble those of Hybrid Tea roses and are suitable for cutting. If dis-budded early, you would need an expert to tell the difference between the two.

Polyantha Roses

Polyanthas came into prominence in the 1930s and 1940s when florists began growing them in pots as gifts for Easter and Mother's Day. The most popular cultivars are Cecile Brunner, Cameo,

Margo Koster, Mothersday, Dopey, The Fairy, China Doll, Happy, and Sparkler. They produce a greater profusion of bloom and far longer bloom period than any other rose. They come in various bush sizes ranging in height from 16 to 36 inches (40 to 90 cm). Another distinct type in this class is the Dwarf Polyantha growing from 12 to 18 inches (30 to 45 cm). These produce flowers in compact clusters from stems of different stages of maturity which ensures a steady supply of flowers. The blooms are small and do not exceed 2 inches (5 cm) in diameter.

English Roses

English roses are a new group of roses developed by David Austin of England. These roses combine the best of the Old Garden roses and Modern roses that produce classic flower forms, fragrance, repeat bloom, and disease resistance. We see many of these roses being sold. Some of the more common varieties are Graham Thomas, Heritage, L.D. Braithwaite, Abraham Darby, and Mary

Climbing and rambling roses

Rose Gardening at the Shewchuk Residence

by G.W. Shewchuk

For purposes of illustration, let's review some of the problems the author has to deal with. We have a large rose bed on the east side of our house with good wind protection. The roses get sunlight for a bit more than eight hours per day, but are bothered by tree roots from the neighbor's Black Poplar and Birch, my apple tree, a Linden, and a Bur Oak.

Roses on the south side of our house, in a narrow bed between the house and the concrete driveway, get a full day's sunlight. Protection from inclement weather is adequate, but the heat from the sun is much greater than in beds in more open areas. This bed requires watering twice as often as the others. Because of the extra heat they receive, this is where I find the first appearance of spider mite infestation. In winter when we get mild spells and again in early spring, it is difficult to maintain the snow cover needed to protect tender roses in this location.

In spite of the problems we have with roses on the south side of the house, we are rewarded by getting blossoms one or two weeks earlier than from the beds in other locations. In the fall, these roses are still in bloom two to three weeks after the frost has nipped the other beds. Taking these extra two-week periods together, we get an additional month of blooming. The bonus of an extra month is tremendously appreciated in the shorter growing season on the plains and prairies.

Our third rose bed is a fairly long one at the front (west side) of the house, about 10 feet (3 m) away. This bed came out of a portion of our front lawn. All available space at the back of our house (east) was taken up with established roses, and it became impossible to find space for additional good roses we saw and heard of, or the new ones that were introduced each year. It was difficult to resist planting some beautiful rose that we did not already have. That is how our front lawn keeps getting smaller and the rose beds larger.

In our front bed the roses get sunlight for approximately 11 hours per day, which is more than sufficient. They also take the brunt of most of the storms that nature thrusts upon them. On a couple of occasions, these roses have taken a terrific beating in a wind or hail storm. The rose canes were thrashed about, leaves shredded, and flowers strewn across the garden. The amazing ability of roses to recover has been repeatedly demonstrated – a week after the storm, all appeared normal, and you would never have guessed what they had gone through.

Rose. Cultural requirements in our area are the same as for the more tender roses, although they are listed in this book with the Shrub roses.

Climbing and Rambler Roses

In mild climates, Climbing and Rambler roses are grown to cover walls and arches or, because of their long climbing branches, to form backgrounds and screens.

Some of the best examples of Climbing roses on the plains and prairies are subjected to special care by their owners. In late fall, the canes are carefully taken off the trellis, wall, fence, or archway and curled on the ground around the base. Then the canes are weighted down with bricks or rocks and covered with a little soil. On top of this, 2 feet (60 cm) of potato tops, lawn clippings, leaves, and other garden material that can be picked up in the process of a fall garden clean-up are added. Considerable care must be taken to avoid breaking the canes because Climbing roses generally bloom on last year's growth.

The cultivars Blaze, Danse du Feu (Spectacular), Morning Jewel, Compassion, Goldstar, Salita, and Rosarium Uetersen appear to be the hardiest of the Climbers. Patricia Macoun is the hardiest of the Ramblers. Explorer roses such as John Cabot can be treated as Climbers.

Miniature Roses

Miniature roses are everblooming replicas of Hybrid Teas that can be as small as the tip of your little finger to about 1½ inch (3 to 4 cm) across. Plant sizes vary from 6 to 18 inches (15 to 45 cm) in height. Despite their small size, they are as easy to overwinter outdoors as the Hybrid Teas if you follow our recommended methods. If not already in pots, they can also be potted up and moved indoors for winter, as they will do well there. If you have numerous Miniatures outdoors, and because they

Mini orange cascade

Shape of flowers

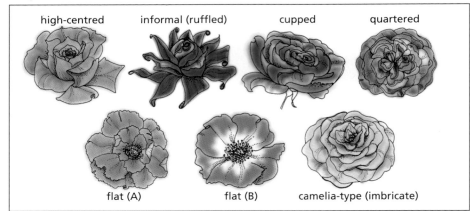

high-centred   informal (ruffled)   cupped   quartered

flat (A)   flat (B)   camelia-type (imbricate)

are so petite, large numbers can be also be stored in a root cellar or basement cold room. Their use in the landscape is usually limited to special purposes because Miniatures are not noted for fragrance, and are of such small size.

Moss Roses

Moss roses get their name from the tiny hair-like glands that cover the sepals and sometimes the terminal parts of stems that resemble moss. This growth is sticky and gives off a resinous aroma like that of balsam fir. They range in size from 3 to 6 feet (1 to 2 m) down to the 6-inch (15-cm) Miniatures.

Shrub Roses

Many Shrub roses are able to survive our winters without any special protection and therefore are characterized by their hardiness. This class is used rather loosely. Rosarians use it as a "catch-all" for cultivars that do not fit in any of the commonly recognized classes. Shrub roses vary in size (depending on the cultivar) up to 6 feet (2 m) in height. Many of the older cultivars bloom only once during the spring. Newly developed cultivars bloom almost continuously from spring until fall. They include the Rugosa cultivars, plus the Hybrid Foetida, Hybrid Spinosissima, Old Garden roses, Explorer roses, English roses, and the many other hybrids related to the Japanese and Altai rose.

Shrub roses are commonly used in combination with other shrubs in landscaping. They can be given the same general care as the other shrubs and do not require any special planting method.

Sweetheart Roses

In this type of rose, the individual florets show the perfection of form of the Hybrid Tea rose but are very much smaller. A typical cultivar in this category

is the Polyantha, Cecile Brunner. There are currently many Miniature roses that also may fall into this category.

Standard Tree Roses

Standard Tree roses are usually Hybrid Tea, Floribunda, Grandiflora, or Miniature roses grafted onto a tall briar stock about 3 feet (1 m) from the ground. This gives the appearance of a small tree.

Standard Tree Rose

graft union

3 to 4 feet (1 metre)

Potted roses

A similar approach with Miniatures grafted onto a shorter stock 1 to 2 feet (30 to 60 cm) in height yields a dwarf style Standard Tree rose.

Guide To Buying Roses

You can never know how well a rose will do simply by looking at the pictures on the package or in the catalogue. There is general agreement that the best way to choose your roses is to see them growing in your neighborhood or in local garden centers. Attending rose shows can be very helpful in selecting rose types, colors, or cultivars that you like.

A very useful guide to assist in rose selection is Chapter 4, Summary of Rose Characteristics. Familiarize yourself with the legend at the end of the table for a description of the abbreviations used within the table.

The first requirement for successful rose growing is to purchase plants of good quality. You can be quite confident of getting strong, healthy, well-rooted plants if you buy them by mail order from any of the major, reputable rose nurseries (see Mail Order Suppliers in the Resource Materials section). These nurseries pack the dormant bushes in a water-proof wrapping which keeps them from drying out. Generally you will receive them in top shape.

You may have noticed that the small packaged roses are not as common as they used to be. Quite common now in

**Packaged roses
(unpruned vs. pruned roots)**

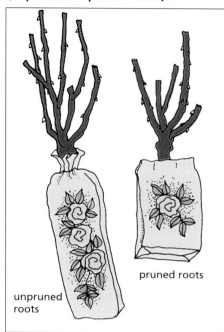

pruned roots

unpruned roots

garden centers are roses in 2 gallon (around 10 L) containers. Generally these are a good buy provided the staff at these centers have given them adequate water and fertilizer during the sales period.

What you get in the small containers are bushes with severely pruned roots. Given a choice between the amputated roots in a small box with a handful of wood shavings or peat and one with most of its roots intact, take the latter even if you have to pay double or triple the price. No reliable nursery would deliberately cut 75 percent of the roots off its trees and shrubs. They know that good roots are essential for getting the plant off to a good start. In the short season and harsh climate on the northern plains and prairies, roses must have as much of their roots intact as possible. From personal experience and scientific research, rose growers know that plants with a good root system take much less time to get established and bloom than those with a severely cropped root system. The American Rose Magazine recently listed several rose societies that

Roses with pruned roots

Roses with unpruned roots

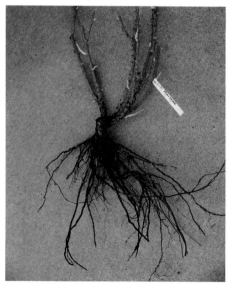

complained about this problem and threatened to boycott firms that practice heavy root pruning.

If you are going to buy packaged roses, purchase them as soon as they arrive at the dealers. If it is too early for planting, pot them in 2 gallon (10 L) containers. They can be stored safely when the weather is bad and put out when the sun shines. When it is safe to do so, they can be transplanted outdoors.

If you have to purchase heavily root-pruned roses to get a particular variety that you can't get otherwise, purchase them early with the buds just starting and sprouts no longer than ½ inch (12 mm). If planted in 2 gallon (10 L) containers, and given special care for the entire growing season, the rose will likely have the container filled with roots. It can then be safely overwintered as described in the section Overwintering Potted Roses. A fully rooted plant stands a better chance of surviving the rigors of exposure in a rose bed when planted the following spring.

Each spring, many firms get on the gardening bandwagon by selling roses, other selected ornamentals, and bedding plants. Also, thousands of plants are ruined by inexperienced, careless, and uninformed management and sales people. Often rose bushes are put on exhibit outdoors for sale in early spring and in a few days are dead from repeated freezing and thawing. To the amazement of knowledgeable gardeners, these dead roses are held on display and sold to unwary customers long after their demise. Is it any wonder that people tell you they just cannot grow roses, or that they are reluctant to try growing them again?

Many people who scorn buying day-old bread or wilted lettuce, will deliberately postpone buying roses until the clearance sale day. By this time many of the plants will have suffered and dried out beyond any hope of a healthy recovery. Many may also have begun to leaf out or produce long, slender, pale green sprouts. A plant in this condition is not a prime specimen. You cannot grow quality blooms from inferior stock.

Knowledgeable managers of retail outlets know that packaged roses are perishable, and develop well-planned facilities to provide proper care and display areas. In addition, informed personnel properly care for the plants until they are sold. These are the only outlets that the shrewd rose gardener should patronize.

A healthy rose plant has a green, plump appearance. Do not confuse the green wax protective coating with the appearance of a healthy plant. The plant should have at least three hefty stems of reasonable length. The buds should be plainly visible. The bark on the canes should not be wrinkled or withered. Ideally, there should be no sprouts longer than ½ inch (12 mm) or any indication of sprouts having been removed.

Rose Grades

Another guide for buying roses often overlooked or not known to many is grade. Rose bushes are graded just like eggs, butter, or potatoes. A No. 1 grade rose carries three or more stout 18-inch (45-cm) canes. A No. 1.5 grade rose has two, 15-inch (38-cm) canes, and a No. 2 rose has two, 12-inch (30-cm) canes. Quite common on the market are ungraded roses marked, "two year old, field grown". If you have a choice, No. 1 grade is generally the best buy.

Importance of Waxing

If there is a choice between roses with waxed canes or unwaxed canes, choose the waxed specimens. Waxing helps to prevent the rapid dehydration that can occur from the time they are packaged to the time they are planted. Tests conducted in the United States have proven that bushes with waxed canes consistently out perform the unwaxed specimens. They establish themselves much faster and produce more blossoms. This effect is evident even in the second year of growth.

Sprouted Roses

Avoid buying heavily sprouted roses. Retailers often receive their rose shipment with sprouts of up to 6 inches (15 cm) on their plants. It then requires a crew of employees to hastily take them off to ready them for sale. It often takes a rose gardener with considerable experience to detect bushes that have had their sprouts removed.

Hybrid Tea rose grades

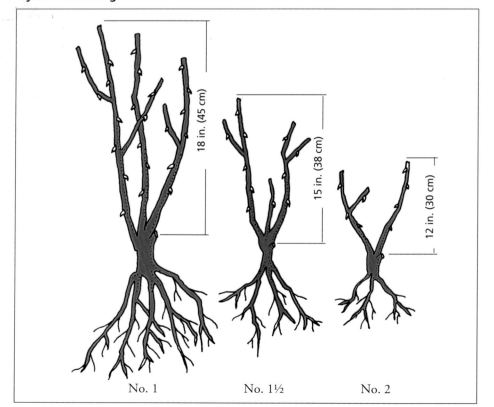

18 in. (45 cm)   15 in. (38 cm)   12 in. (30 cm)

No. 1   No. 1½   No. 2

Avoid planting rose bushes with sprouts longer than 2 inches (5 cm). If you have no choice, remove the sprouts prior to planting them. This is not necessarily the best thing for the rose bush, but it is the lesser of two evils. You can remove the sprouts and allow the bush to expend its remaining energy on "new shoots", or leave the sprouts on and have the bush expend much of its energy on sprouts it may eventually lose anyway.

The tender sprouts need as much protection as possible from frost, wind, heat, or sun-scald. The sprouts need to be hardened off so they can withstand these natural elements without injury. This can be easily done by covering them with a burlap sack. This porous cover is retained for a week to ten days during which time the sprouts green up. Remove the cover for short periods on cloudy, calm, or rainy days to permit gradual adjustment. When fully greened up, the cover can be permanently removed.

Some people prefer to protect and harden off their rose bushes by mounding the bushes with soil when they are planted. When the sprouts begin to appear through the mound, the soil can be gradually removed to get the shoots hardened off fully.

Potted Roses

A safer way for the novice to buy roses is to choose specimens that are already potted. You can tell at a glance whether or not the bush is growing and healthy in appearance. Another advantage is that they may be planted in late spring or summer, when planting of dormant bushes is neither feasible nor practical. Potted roses can be stored in a safe place until the risk of frost is gone. On the other hand, they cost more and offer no other particular advantage if planting can be done in early spring.

Good Cultivars To Start With

Each year new roses are being added to the already comprehensive list of nearly 16,000 cultivars, and older mediocre cultivars are being downgraded by thousands of rose growers throughout the United States. Keep in mind that rose performance rating changes with time. However, some like Peace, Chrysler Imperial, and Queen Elizabeth have been around for more than twenty-five years and are still looked upon as top roses. Over the last few years, however, many newly introduced roses are giving them a good run for their money. Also in the field of new roses are cultivars resistant to mildew, blackspot, and severe winter conditions.

Hybridists at government research stations, as well as some independent American and Canadian horticulturists, have developed a number of very hardy shrub roses for the harsh northern plains and prairie weather. Some of the varieties are: Adelaide Hoodless, Cuthbert Grant, Morden Centennial, Morden Fireglow, Morden Blush, Morden Ruby, Hope for Humanity, Winnipeg Parks, Prairie Dawn, Prairie Joy, Jens Munk, many Explorer roses, Kakwa, and several Bugnet roses. These cultivars came through our severe winters without the special planting and wintering instructions outlined here for tender roses.

Hardiness and winter survival in tender roses (besides the method of planting and winter cover recommended here) depend largely on the rootstock. In the rose nursery trade many varieties of roses are used for the rootstock. Many of these are not hardy on the northern plains and prairies and other colder areas. It is unfortunate for us that many of these roses are stocked and sold by some of our garden shops.

Some nurseries that propagate roses mention the variety of rootstock they use. The common hardy rootstocks for our climate are *Rosa canina* and *Rosa multiflora*. There are several rose catalogs

in the Resource Materials section from the United States, Scotland, England, Germany, and Canada which state the rootstock they use.

Another choice is getting roses grown from cuttings called own-root roses. Several companies in the United States and Canada specialize in the production of own-root roses. These nurseries are listed in the Mail Order Suppliers section in the back of this book.

Keeping the above factors in mind when purchasing roses will assure you of better winter survival.

What roses should you plant? This is a personal thing. Some like to show, others like cut roses for the house, and others wish to have roses in the landscape. Do your own thing with the full spectrum of roses. In Chapter 4, Summary of Rose Characteristics, you will find a short listing of good roses that you can rely on for performance and beauty.

The column labelled "George's Choice" includes proven roses that have done well over a period of years for many people throughout the plains and prairies.

Sources of Good Roses

The best place to purchase roses is from a reputable mail order supply house. It is best to order early when the supply is plentiful so that you do not have to accept substitutes. The best time to order your roses is before the end of the year and not later than January. You should also request that they be shipped when danger of hard frost is over, to arrive some time between April 15 and 30 in the northern United States and Canada.

Some of the quality mail order suppliers are listed in the Resource Materials section. If you are considering importing roses, the procedure is also outlined in the Resource Materials section.

In this highly competitive business, there are some very reputable local garden centers. Gardeners should patronize them. Here, the plants get the best of care, and the personnel are knowledgeable and can offer sound advice.

If you intend to purchase roses at a local gardening supply outlet, make certain that you get them as soon as the shipment arrives. If necessary, you can possibly hold your roses for a week or two by following the instructions given under the Heeling In and Potted Rose sections. As mentioned earlier, do not buy roses with dried canes or long sprouts even if they are reduced to clear.

The Best Roses

What are the best roses? This is a very difficult question to answer. Perhaps the best way to answer this is to consult Chapter 4. In particular, review the cultivars identified as "Author's Choice".

Soil and Roses

Roses generally grow well in any soil that produces good vegetables. Roses also grow under a great variety of undesirable soil types and conditions, but you cannot expect them to produce to the best of their potential. Roses cannot tolerate poor drainage, or unduly alkaline or acid soil.

Drainage

Good drainage is essential to rose growing. Roses require soil that is absorbent enough to retain adequate moisture for vigorous growth, but they do not like wet feet.

Avoid planting roses in areas where water from rain and snow melt is likely to accumulate. In areas of poor drainage, try raised beds. If this doesn't work, install drainage tile, or grow them in containers.

Texture

Friable sandy, clay loam is just right for roses. It has the capability of draining away excess water and still retaining sufficient moisture for good plant growth.

This soil texture has a fair amount of clay with enough organic matter and coarse sand in the right proportions to make an absorbent, friable soil that crumbles easily and does not pack or dry like cement. A handful of this soil, when slightly moist and compressed, falls apart when you open your hand. You cannot make soil balls with good garden soil.

Heavy clay can be made workable and more productive by the incorporation of coarse sand, vermiculite, perlite, or organic matter. The organic matter can be in the form of well rotted cow manure, coarse peat moss, or compost. Coarse

sand should look the size of cracked wheat. The addition of fine sand could make a heavy clay soil as hard as an adobe brick when dry.

Very sandy soil, which can result in droughty conditions and loose soil structure, can be improved by incorporating some clay and organic matter. It may take as much as 3 inches (7 to 8 cm) of peat moss or other organic matter worked into the upper foot (30 cm) of topsoil to improve this soil.

Soil Reaction

Most home gardeners are familiar with using commercial fertilizers to improve soil fertility. However, very few are familiar with the pH factor and how it affects soils and plant growth.

Roses do best in a soil with a pH reading of 6.0 to 6.5. This is slightly acidic. A neutral soil would have a pH reading of 7.0. Alkaline soil would have a pH higher than 7.0. For the purpose of comparison, the pH value of some common household substances and food items are listed below:

Item	pH
Pure lemon juice	2.0
Vinegar	2.2
Tomatoes	4.2
Milk	6.6
Baking soda	8.2
Milk of magnesia	10.5
Pure alkali (lye)	14.0

Although roses will tolerate a wider pH range than 6.0 to 6.5, it is best to provide them with optimum conditions.

Roses subjected to undesirable pH levels are likely to suffer nutritional problems. The pH can be determined by using a soil test kit available from most garden supply shops although most commercially available garden kits can produce highly variable results. Sending samples to a soil testing laboratory is the most reliable method. If you request it, a complete analysis of your soil can be carried out showing available nitrogen, phosphorus, and potassium, plus micronutrients and special factors such as pH and salinity. If requested, they will also provide recommendations for adjusting the pH of your particular soil.

A gardener can change the pH reading of garden soil to any desired acidic or alkaline level. The addition of lime will raise the pH level making it more alkaline. Powdered sulfur will lower the pH, as will the addition of peat moss which usually has a pH of 4.5 to 5.0.

In a few years your soil pH reading may return to its previous level due to leaching. Therefore, you need to check the acidity every couple of years, and determine whether your soil pH needs adjusting.

Where only a few rose bushes are involved and there is a high soil pH reading (alkaline), aluminum sulfate can be used on each individual plant. This acidifier can be obtained at most garden shops. The container generally has instructions for its use.

Conversely, if the soil pH is lower than 6 (acidic), adding dolomite lime in the area of the plant will raise the pH. Exercise caution and don't overdo a good thing. It is best to treat lightly, test, and re-treat if necessary.

Preparing Roses For Planting

Whether you receive your roses from a mail order supplier or purchase them from a local garden center, you can take certain steps to get your roses off to a good start.

Basic Care

The first step in preparing your roses for planting is to soak their roots in water, for one or two days. A weak solution of 20-20-20 fertilizer and water can also be used, but read the label carefully for mixing instructions. This is usually about one-third of the recommended strength. Never allow "bare root" roses to remain packed for more than a day or two even if you are not ready to plant them or the weather is not co-operating.

Heeling In

If the rose plants you ordered arrive before you are ready, or the weather does not permit planting, they can be stored safely for up to two weeks by using the following procedure:
- Dig a trench 2 feet (60 cm) deep in a shady sheltered place.
- Spread the rose plants out in the trench after they have received a good soaking (see Basic Care).
- Lay them out at a 45 degree angle and then cover with moist soil, peat moss, or sawdust. Leave the top quarter of the canes showing above ground. It is much easier to dig out roses as needed when moist peat moss is used.
- Water them well.

Should there be a threat of frost, protect the tops with a burlap sacking, straw, or some other light covering.

Cold Storage

A root cellar or cold storage room is also a good place to store boxed or packaged rose bushes. However, make sure that they have adequate moisture. If the packing material is dry, add water.

Soaking roses before planting

Heeling in

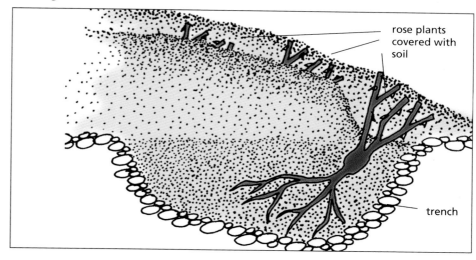

rose plants covered with soil

trench

Planting New Plants

There is more to planting roses than just digging a hole, sticking a rose plant into it, and covering the roots with soil. In this section you will discover some of the most important steps to be taken to ensure the survival of your rose plants through winter and into spring.

Timing

The best time to plant roses in the average year on the northern American plains is between April 15 and 30. On the Canadian prairies it is usually between April 25 and May 15. Quite often during this period it is windy, hot and dry; this is not very conducive to the establishment of tender plants. Plant in the late afternoon, and be prepared to give the new plants the opportunity to regain some of the energy lost through digging, shipping, and exposure. In other words, "care" for them. In general, it is desirable to plant as early in the spring as possible.

Planting Method

Planting properly has different meanings in various parts of the United States and Canada. This is obvious when the planting instructions are read on packaged roses from different parts of the continent. The uncertainty is not at all reduced by reading the numerous manuals on the market.

In the cool agricultural areas of the northern plains and prairies, the planting method described here is the secret to the successful growing of Hybrid Tea, Grandiflora, Polyantha, Floribunda, and the tender Shrub roses. Apply the following procedures and savor the splendor of beautiful, vigorous roses.

Dig holes at least 18 inches (45 cm) deep. Replace the soil, if poor, with a rich garden loam or with a mixture of:
- one part peat moss and/or compost
- one part perlite, coarse sand, or vermiculite (vermiculite breaks down quite quickly in comparison to perlite)
- one part garden soil.

The addition of 1 cup (250 mL) of bonemeal per plant is also beneficial.

When the hole is dug and the fill soil is prepared, place a small board or cane horizontally across the middle of the hole to mark the surface level. Spread out the roots and position the plant so that the graft union is 4 inches (10 cm) below the marker. Hold the pre-soaked rose in this position as the hole is filled. Firm the soil around the roots. In the planting illustration, note the position and depth. If you are planting packaged or boxed

roses with their normally amputated roots, there is little problem positioning the roots during planting. Bushes with such very short root stocks make planting in a vertical position appropriate. The graft union is readily positioned at the 4-inch (10-cm) depth.

Under normal conditions, rose roots penetrate to a depth of 18 inches (45 cm); the majority of the roots are concentrated in the 6- to 12-inch (15-to 30-cm) soil depth zone. Plants react negatively to being planted either too deep or too shallow. Long rooted bushes may need the canes and roots positioned at a 45 degree angle in order to have the majority of roots concentrated at the optimal depth, and the graft union at 4 inches (10 cm). This is shown in the illustrations on this page.. When new shoots appear, they will assume the normal vertical position, and the old angled stems will not be noticeable.

You will notice in the Recommended Planting Method illustration that, after covering the roots, coarse aggregate (perlite, coarse sand, or vermiculite) is heaped over the graft union. This is done specifically to assist new shoots from the graft union and the canes underground to easily penetrate the soil. In the event that all top growth is killed, the most vital parts of the rose plant can still send up shoots through this coarse material without too much difficulty. You will also note that a "saucer-like" depression is left around each plant for easy watering. The graft is actually 2 inches (5 cm) below the depression surface and 4 inches (10 cm) below surface level. Immediately after planting, give the rose bushes a thorough, deep soaking by filling up the depression several times.

Allow plenty of room around each rose. Plant Hybrid Teas, Grandifloras, and Floribundas about 2 to 2½ feet (60 to 75 cm) apart. For Miniatures, use half that distance.

Recommended planting method

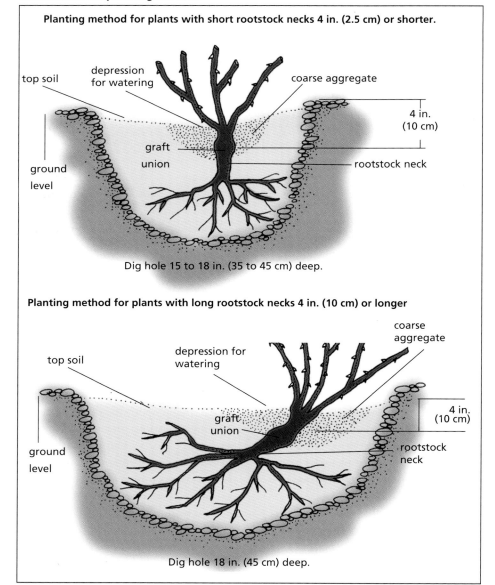

Planting method for plants with short rootstock necks 4 in. (2.5 cm) or shorter.

top soil — depression for watering — coarse aggregate

ground level

graft union — rootstock neck

4 in. (10 cm)

Dig hole 15 to 18 in. (35 to 45 cm) deep.

Planting method for plants with long rootstock necks 4 in. (10 cm) or longer

top soil — depression for watering — coarse aggregate

ground level

graft union — rootstock neck

4 in. (10 cm)

Dig hole 18 in. (45 cm) deep.

Roses: A Gardener's Guide for the Plains and Prairies

Protecting Newly Planted Roses

Newly planted rose bushes must be protected against dehydration. It takes two or three weeks after planting under good growing conditions for new roots to form. This is a critical time for the weakened plant. A common way of protecting rose plants is to make cylinders out of heavy building paper about 12 inches (30 cm) tall and 12 inches (30 cm) in diameter. To prevent the cylinder from shifting, staple it to a wooden stake inserted into the soil along its side. Place the cylinder over the plant and fill with a mixture of soil and peat moss. Keep it moist but do not overwater. Leave the paper collar in place until new growth appears. Remove the cylinder and gradually lower the mound of soil giving the new growth time to harden off.

Some people simply hill up newly planted roses to the tips of the canes and achieve the same thing. Hilling can also be done using mulch or other insulating material. The mulching material is gradually removed when new shoots begin to show through, making sure that the "saucer-like" depression needed for watering is recreated.

Another simple method of protecting rose plants after planting and watering in, is to cover the bushes with burlap sacking for a week to ten days. During that period uncover only when appropriate, such as when it is gently raining or very calm and cloudy. Under such cover the sprouts green up and harden-off to withstand the sun and drying wind. This method eliminates the chore of obtaining, storing, and disposing of a protective soil covering.

If you protect your rose bushes immediately after planting, you will be rewarded with a bumper crop of beautiful blooms.

Planting A Potted Rose Bush

To plant a potted rose bush, dig a hole twice the diameter and twice the

Protecting newly planted roses

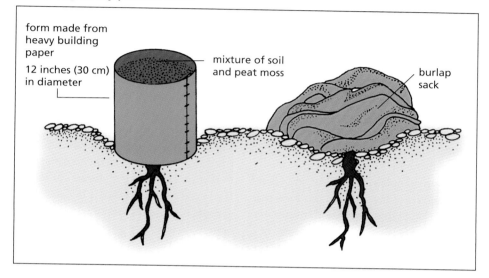

form made from heavy building paper 12 inches (30 cm) in diameter — mixture of soil and peat moss — burlap sack

depth of the pot. Then remove the plant from the pot. Roses purchased in plastic pots slip out very easily if the soil is a bit dry. If this is not the case, cut vertically down the pot in two or three places without disturbing the roots. Carefully tear away the pot so as to not damage the root ball. Partially fill the hole with good soil, making certain that when the unpotted plant is set in the hole, the graft union will be 4 inches (10 cm) below ground level. Now fill the rest of the hole around the root ball with good soil. Firm up the soil and form a shallow dish 2 inches (5 cm) deep around the rose canes. Fill with water several times to thoroughly soak the soil.

Planting Climbing Roses

The same method of planting is used for Climbing roses as for the Hybrid Tea, Grandiflora, and Floribunda roses with the following exceptions:
* The hardy Climbing roses marked "4" in the "Hardiness" column in Selected Roses, Chapter 4.
* Those marked "2" or "3" in the "Hardiness" column should be planted with canes and rootstock positioned at a 45 degree slant in the direction that you intend to lay it on the ground for winter protection. The reason for this is that you need to preserve and

protect the old canes. Bloom on Climbing roses is produced on the previous year's growth. As the canes get older, they become thicker and stiffer, making it difficult to lay them down without breaking at the base. That is why it is necessary to plant new tender Climber canes and rootstock at a 45 degree angle or less. New canes will grow vertically, but yearly bending and laying down makes them less likely to break.

Cover for winter protection is the same as that suggested elsewhere for other tender roses. The only difference is that you will need a long pile to cover the canes. It is a good idea to tie the canes together in several places with twine. This makes it much easier to lay the canes down to the ground and cover them. Heavy rocks and concrete blocks can help hold the canes on the ground.

Planting Miniature Roses

Miniature roses are relatively easy to plant. They are not grafted or budded but grown from cuttings. Their root system is quite small in comparison to larger roses. Plant them about 2 inches (5 cm) deeper than they were in the original containers. In all other aspects, growing Miniatures is very similar to growing larger roses.

Transplanting

Transplanting a rose in full bloom is generally not recommended, but it can be done if you take reasonable care and attention. Water the rose well the day before transplanting to help the soil adhere to the roots. Spray the plant with an anti-desiccant product such as "Wilt-Pruf" or "Cloud Cover" at least several hours before transplanting. Be sure that coverage of both upper and lower leaf surfaces is complete. Wilt-Pruf and Cloud Cover are wax-like, spray-on products that protect plants from excessive transpiration.

Dig up the plant carefully so as to retain as large a root ball as possible. Moving the plant is easier if the root ball is covered with burlap and tied or held firmly.

The anti-desiccant coating will have weathered away by the time the plant has become established. If it is extremely hot, and especially with a dry breeze blowing, the plant should be shaded or screened for a couple of days. Shading can be achieved by using garden stakes 2 to 3 feet (30 to 90 cm) long inserted in the soil and covered by a piece of burlap. If the first few days are cloudy and cool, no protection is necessary.

Replacing Rose Bushes

When planting new roses to replace old or failing bushes, remove all the soil surrounding the root ball of the old bush and replace with new soil. Use the soil mixture recommended under the Planting Method section. If the old bush had root or crown gall, or any other disease, remove twice or even three times as much soil. This should provide a good base for a new rose. If permitted, burn the discarded rose to destroy any harbored diseases or insects. If you can't burn it, place it in a sealed garbage bag and dispose of with other household waste.

Renovating Old Rose Beds

On the plains and prairies more trials and research are needed to determine when it is best to replace old, worn-out plants. Most good rose cultivars remain quite productive for 10 to 12 years, although some have lasted up to 25 to 30 years.

After a number of years, all roses gradually fade. The soil loses productivity, organic matter is lost, and it can become compacted to such an extent that it cannot adequately support a healthy, vigorous plant. Rose production will decline eventually, in spite of the consistent use of sound horticultural practices.

One method of slowing this gradual deterioration is to periodically rebuild the beds when the roses are dormant. Do this as soon as possible after the spring thaw. This may occur in April or early May depending on the weather. The bushes should be carefully dug up and "heeled in" immediately in a sheltered spot. Keep them damp during the renovation period.

Renovation consists of adding organic matter, coarse sand, vermiculite or perlite, and phosphate fertilizer. Then the rose bed is dug and turned over. Organic matter may be peat moss, well-rotted manure, or compost. The proportions of these will vary from garden to garden depending on the type of soil you have. You need to create a fairly loose, loamy soil that will take in water readily but not pack easily. Be certain to add any soil amendments (including sulfur or lime if needed) and the phosphate fertilizer on the soil before the initial digging. Work the fertilizer down into the root zone. A soil analysis will give reliable guidelines as to quantities to use. Phosphorous fertilizer

Container gardening

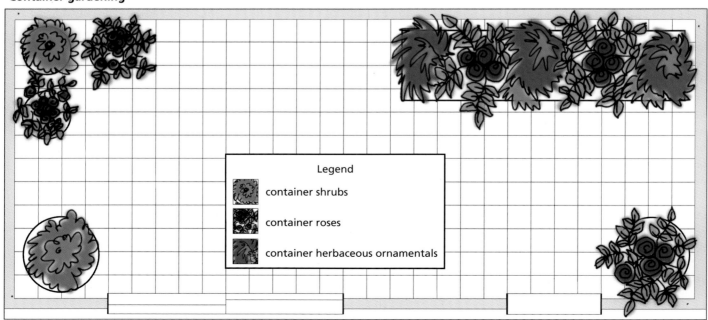

Legend

container shrubs

container roses

container herbaceous ornamentals

does not readily leach downward to the roots when applied to the surface. Now, water the bed well. This allows the bed to firm up sufficiently before the bushes are replanted. The total renovation should be completed within a week to ten days.

Growing Roses In Containers

Whether you have an outdoor garden or not, you can still grow roses. Almost any kind of rose can be grown in a container. Cultivars that are low and bushy are most suitable, but you can try any rose of your choice. The table Roses Suitable for Container Growing on page 5 lists some reliable cultivars that have been grown with success.

Containers for growing the larger roses should be at least 18 to 24 inches (45 to 60 cm) wide and 16 to 24 inches (40 to 60 cm) deep. For Miniatures, 6-inch to 8-inch (15- to 20-cm) diameter pots are suitable. Wood, clay, or plastic containers are all satisfactory. In a pot 24 inches (60 cm) wide and 24 inches (60 cm) deep, you can plant either a Hybrid Tea, three Floribundas or up to twelve Miniatures.

A mix of 1 part peat moss and/or compost, 1 part coarse sand, and 2 parts good garden soil is a suitable soil mixture for roses in containers. For good drainage, place a 1-inch (2.5-cm) layer of gravel in the bottom of the container before planting the roses. Make sure there are adequate drainage holes at the bottom of the container.

A rose is planted in a container in the conventional manner with the graft union just below the surface. Outdoor maintenance instructions given elsewhere in this publication do not apply to container grown roses.

Water is required more frequently than for garden grown roses because of the smaller moisture holding capacity of a pot. For fertilizing suggestions refer to the section on Fertilizing.

Just before fall freeze-up, move the containerized roses into a root house. If a root house is not available, bury them

horizontally in a 2½-foot (75 cm) deep hole in a well drained location where there is likely to be a good snow cover. The soil must be moist. To facilitate easier digging out in spring, use damp peat moss or sawdust for cover rather than the excavated soil. In spring when the soil has thawed sufficiently, the roses can be dug up, pruned, and routine maintenance begun.

Roses that have been grown in the same container for three years require re-potting. Re-potting is best done in the early spring before sprouting begins.

Growing Under Artificial Lights

Miniature roses can be easily grown under fluorescent plant-light bulbs such as Gro-Lux, Vigor Light, Gro-Light, Vita-Lite, Agro-Lite, and others. Some plant-lights are too rich in the red wave lengths and give spindly growth. A 1:1 mix of standard fluorescent cool white and fluorescent plant-lights will usually give good growth. This is also less expensive than using plant-lights only. Metal halide

and high pressure sodium lights work very well. Sun Agro, 430 watt lights provide the closest to natural sunlight available to date. Incandescent plant-light bulbs can also be used, but they create a lot of heat, are expensive to operate, and do not last as long as fluorescent bulbs. Regular household incandescent bulbs are not recommended because they are rich in the red and infra-red light necessary for flowering, but weak in the blue and violet rays necessary for vegetative growth.

Miniatures are particularly suited to indoor growing because they are small, flower continually, have many colors, and are compatible with other house plants.

A temperature of 60 to 70°F (16 to 21°C) is suitable for vegetative growth. Lower temperatures of 40°F (4°C) encourage flower production. Humidity should be between 50 to 60 percent for optimum growth.

Lighting assemblies can be purchased or fabricated. They should have reflectors of polished aluminum or white enamel. Set the lamps 4 inches (10 cm) apart and

Growing under artificial lights

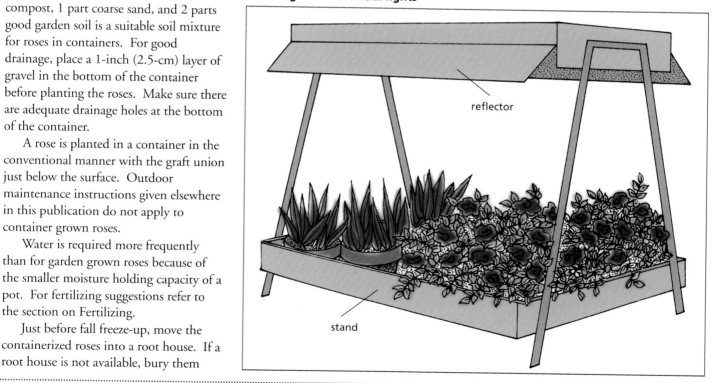

reflector

stand

8 inches (20 cm) above the foliage. The lights should be turned on for 12 to 18 hours per day. An 18-hour light period will force faster growth, but 14 hours is a good average.

Pot sizes should be 3 inches (7.5 cm) for the Miniature roses and up to 6 inches (15 cm) for larger varieties. A soil mix of 2 parts soil, 3 parts vermiculite, and 1 part peat moss and/or compost is considered suitable.

Propagating Roses From Cuttings

There is a lot of controversy over the advantages and disadvantages of roses grown by budding or grafting versus those grown from cuttings. There are those who claim that budded plants produce larger plants with larger flowers, and are generally more vigorous plants. Those who prefer growing roses from cuttings claim that with thousands of cultivars that claim is not accurate, and in fact, roses on their own roots have a better root system, more disease resistance, and in some cases are actually more winter hardy.

Excellent roses can be grown from cuttings taken in October when following the recommended winter protection outlined in this book. Cuttings are then rooted and grown under fluorescent lights over winter. Surprisingly, some bloom by Christmas Day, and in spring they can be planted out to continue their growth. Some of the author's roses produced in this way have done well for ten years.

If you are interested in growing "own-root" roses, the materials you need, and the step-by-step directions can be obtained from the booklet titled, *Successfully Rooting Rose Cuttings*, by David P. Kidger, listed in the Resource Materials section under Reference Materials.

Note: Most of the new rose cultivars are patented. It is illegal to propagate such roses without permission being obtained and royalties paid. A patented plant designation is usually stamped on a metal tag or label attached to the rose. A patent on a rose expires after twenty years unless renewed. There are, however, innumerable roses that are not currently protected by patents.

Use of the symbol ™ indicates a trademark that protects the use of the name of the rose. If ® appears after the name, it designates that the rose is registered with the International Registration Authority for Roses (IRAR) by the International Society for Horticultural Science.

Maintenance

Once your roses are planted and growing, there are a few routine chores to complete that will enhance their productivity throughout the growing season. You will find the most important of these chores outlined in the following section.

Late Spring Frost Protection

When a late spring frost is predicted, sprouted roses must be protected with some type of cover. Burlap or newspapers provide good protection, but they must be anchored down to prevent winds from blowing them away. Fiber pots (if you have any) are good protectors. Another method is to set out a sprinkler to cover the desired area. Start the sprinkler just as the temperature reaches the freezing point and leave it on until the temperature returns to above freezing. The critical point often comes one or two hours before sunrise. Overall coverage of the rose bed is necessary for this method to be effective.

Cultivation

Cultivation is routinely necessary to control weeds, prevent diseases, and loosen up the surface soil. Roughing up the soil surface makes it more open to moisture penetration, and helps to develop a more friable growing medium. Deep cultivation is not recommended because shallow rose roots may be injured.

Watering

Rose bushes grow best when they receive an average of 1 inch (2.5 cm) of moisture per week during the hot dry periods of the plains and prairie growing season. There are times when there is very little rainfall. Supplementary watering is necessary during these periods. A rain gauge or a couple of shallow pans placed in the rose bed are necessary to determine how much supplementary water is actually required to make up any shortage when overhead sprinklers are used. An application of 6 to 7 gallons (25 L) per plant approximates 1 inch (2.5 cm) of rain over the entire garden when each rose bush is watered individually by hand.

Roses respond amazingly to adequate feeding and watering. You can avoid periods of reduced flower production if you water and fertilize well.

There are several methods of watering roses. One method is to use an overhead sprinkler. However, this wets the foliage, and wet foliage encourages the spread of diseases such as black spot, rust, and mildew. This can be overcome by doing the overhead sprinkling early in the morning, which allows the foliage to dry off quickly before it becomes hot in the sun. Sprinkling the entire bed can be a waste of water and ineffective in getting water directly to the roots, unless you have a perfectly level rose bed. A soaker hose can be used but it takes a long time, and, depending on the equipment, it can be difficult to determine how much water has been applied.

The following method is reasonably fast and effective. After the rose bushes are uncovered in the spring, contour the soil around each plant and form a saucer 2 inches (5 cm) deep and 12 to 18 inches (30 to 45 cm) in diameter, as recommended when planting new roses. Be careful not to expose the roots. A bit of sawdust or peat moss mulch in this depression will prevent rapid evaporation and retain moisture. The saucer-like depression at the base of each bush facilitates easier watering, and it brings the graft union nearer the surface, making it easier for new shoots to emerge.

A 4-foot (1.2-m) watering wand with a water breaker head provides easy access to bushes up to 6 feet (2 m) away. Travel up and down the rows filling each saucer-like depression with water. By the time you reach the end, the first ones are ready to receive another filling. Refill each "saucer" repeatedly until you have given close to 6 or 7 gallons (25 L) of water to each individual bush. Actually measure it out the first time to be sure you are applying the correct amount. With this method, every plant gets plenty of water where it is needed most—throughout the root system.

Fertilizing

Newly planted roses should not be fertilized until new growth is 2 to 3 inches (5 to 7.5 cm) long.

Roses are heavy feeders and their performance, to a great extent, depends on soil fertility and the moisture supply. When the soil is workable in the spring, start the season with an ample helping of up to 2 inches (5 cm) of well-rotted cow manure or other organic matter. This is easily incorporated shallowly into the surface soil with a garden fork. Then, begin regular light feedings with a balanced, readily soluble fertilizer with trace elements. Nutrients do not become available to the roots unless they are in solution. Therefore, plenty of water makes the whole process work.

For regular feedings, use a water soluble rose fertilizer such as 20-24-14 or 28-14-14. It is also advisable to add liquid fish fertilizer to the fertilizer mix. Follow the recommendations on the containers according to the following schedules:
- May 15
- June 30
- July 31

The above schedule and fertilizer is used until the last application of the year, which should be from mid- to late-August. It is intended to help mature and harden off the plants before the cold weather sets in. Fertilizers such as 10-30-20 can be used. If this is not available, 10-52-10 is a fair substitute but is low in potassium. This is a bit too high in nitrogen and can encourage tender vegetative grown. The high phosphorus encourages maturity, and the potassium strengthens the plant cell wall and prepares it for winter. If you have the agricultural formulations of 11-48-0 and 0-0-60 on hand, prepare your own by mixing two parts of 11-48-0 and one part of 0-0-60. Any of these preparations may be used at the rate of 1 tablespoon of the blended mixture in about 5 quarts (4.5 L) of water for each rose bush.

One alternative to dissolving commercial fertilizers in water is to apply them dry and water them in. This method does not distribute it as evenly and effectively as fertilizer applied in solution.

Once a year, preferably in the spring, add micronized iron to the fertilizer mix (follow label instructions). This is insurance against rose bushes becoming anemic or chlorotic. Iron deficiency is quite common in roses, especially when grown in soil with a pH of 7.5 or higher, and an excess of lime or phosphorus. This condition is aggravated by excessive use of unbalanced fertilizers and high calcium water. A high calcium content is common in many prairie well water and city supply systems. Iron deficiency symptoms are:
- Yellowing of new foliage that later turns cream colored
- Mature leaves that are yellow with dark green veins.

Some rose enthusiasts use "cow tea" to fertilize their roses. "Cow tea" is made in a large barrel. Add cow manure (reasonably fresh – not rotted) and water to the barrel at a ratio of about 1 part manure to 19 parts water, stirring thoroughly. Other livestock manure can also be used. In a week the "cow tea" is ready to use. Keep the barrel covered so the neighbors won't take offence at the stench. After about three fillings, the barrel will need to be recharged with fresh manure. Be careful not to overdo a good thing. Dilute full strength "cow tea" with water until it has the appearance of weak tea.

A good substitute for this is two cups of alfalfa meal per plant per year. "Alfalfa tea" is also a good, odorless substitute for

Fertilizing – Another Approach

In 1980, to experiment, the author fed his roses twice as often at half the rate. It seemed to make sense and the roses appeared to appreciate it, but it did take more time. The recommended fertilizer solution was used at one-half the rate according to the following time schedule:
- May 15
- June 15
- June 30
- July 15
- July 31

The larger, older bushes were given an extra quart (litre) or so of the fertilizer solution each time they were fertilized. This is the schedule that he currently uses.

cow tea. Make it by adding alfalfa pellets to water at a ratio of 1 part alfalfa pellets to 19 parts water and soaking for about three days. Give each rose bush about 5 quarts (4.5 L) of alfalfa tea first thing in the spring and again a month later. The alfalfa leaves that are left at the bottom of your container are still good for another mix. Top up the container with the correct proportion of water and in three days you have more alfalfa tea. It sounds like a more sanitary idea, and the roses seem to benefit from it. You will not have to put up with a big barrel and the manure stench.

There are a few proponents of foliar feeding, and each year somebody says that he has found the answer to quick and inexpensive fertilization. It is inexpensive because very small amounts of nutrients are used in the water spray. This method cannot provide all the requirements, however, because roses are heavy feeders. There is also the risk of burning the foliage if the solution is too strong. Foliar feeding can only effectively supply the micronutrients such as iron, manganese, and magnesium which are required in very small quantities.

Micronutrient Deficiency

Chlorosis (yellowing of leaves) may be caused by a lack of iron or manganese in the soil. This can be the result of years of cropping without replacing these essential elements or growing roses in alkaline soil. Iron and manganese supplements can be obtained from garden supply shops. Deficiency of nitrogen can also cause yellowing of the leaves. Check the nitrogen level and the pH (alkalinity or acidity) of the soil.

For soils deficient in magnesium, or in rose beds older than three years, annually add one tablespoon of Epsom Salt (magnesium sulfate) per plant in a water solution, in addition to the regular feeding. Heavy rains and the use of alkaline city water seem to deplete the availability of magnesium so essential for growth. A magnesium deficient plant

may have chlorotic older leaves which can develop into a brilliant yellow. The chlorosis (yellowing) often start at the tips and moves inwards. Interveinal chlorosis similar to iron and magnesium deficiency makes it difficult to pinpoint the exact deficient nutrient. This can accurately be determined by a soil test. Check the labels of your fertilizers for trace elements. Good soluble fertilizers normally carry enough trace elements to avoid this.

Mulching

If your garden has good soil that retains adequate moisture, plus good drainage, aeration, and a humus balance, it really does not need a mulch. If this is not the case, however, a good mulch will add many more roses to your rose bed.

Mulching can provide the following benefits:
- Permit water and air to pass through easily
- Reduce compaction
- Add humus
- Provide good soil insulation
- Keep the soil and roots cool
- Maintain a high level of moisture
- Prevent soil splattering onto the rose bushes during a rain or watering.

Shredded peat moss provides all these benefits adequately. There are also other mulches that can be used:

- Sawdust
- Wood chips
- Leaves
- Chopped straw and hay
- Tree bark
- Manure.

Mulches should be applied yearly to rose beds to a depth of 1 to 2 inches (2.5 to 5 cm).

Mulch is not a substitute for the water required by roses, but it does reduce moisture loss from the soil surface. A good mulch reduces the number of waterings required. A mulch also serves as an insulator from the intense heat of the sun and helps to maintain a cool and more even soil temperature.

Pat moss can be used as a winter cover, but it is difficult to pick it all up in the spring. Since it makes a good mulch, it is practical to leave some of it on after spring clean-up. If you have access to cheap or free sawdust, do the same with it. However, if sawdust is used and any significant amount remains after spring clean-up, it can reduce available nitrogen. This would necessitate adding more nitrogen in your periodic fertilizer applications. Peat moss and sawdust also look quite presentable in the rose beds and do not produce an unsightly mess if used.

Mulching roses

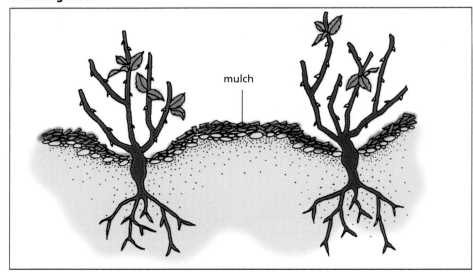

mulch

Basic Pruning

In our cold and extreme weather, very few, if any, tender rose canes survive above the protective winter cover. A protective winter cover is recommended in the Overwintering Roses section. In this case pruning is not urgent. However, there are hardy Shrub roses that send out numerous new canes each year and require annual regenerative pruning.

Shrub rose canes become less productive with age, somewhat like gooseberry and currant bushes. Therefore, it is desirable to encourage the development of new canes. To do this, remove one old cane each year and permit a new one to replace it (see Pruning Roses illustrations). Over time this will eventually produce a shrub with a range of canes from 1 to 5 years old. This is annual maintenance pruning and not corrective pruning for damage or disease control. A shrub rose with 5 to 8 canes makes a nice well-balanced bush. The number depends on the mature size of the bush. Taller bushes may need 7 or 8 canes to show their best.

General Guidelines

Keep these guidelines in mind when pruning (see illustrations):

- Use a good, sharp, scissor-type pruner to get a clean cut. The anvil-type tends to crush the ends of the stems. Dull pruners will mash the stems and such wounds will not seal well and are subject to infection and die-back.
- Remove damaged, diseased, or dead wood. Cut back to sound wood that shows white or greenish pith (the wood within the bark).
- Direct the growth of the canes by making the cut ¼ inch (6 mm) above an eye or leaf bud located in the direction you want the new branch to grow.
- Prune so that the center of the bush is open to the sun and air.
- Remove crossing, twiggy, or frail side growth.
- Leave 5 to 8 healthy canes distributed evenly at the base for shrub roses.

- Look at and study each bush carefully before cutting; once the cane is cut, it cannot be replaced.
- Local climatic conditions dictate the best pruning time. On the northern plains and prairies, this period usually extends from April 20 to early May depending on location and weather conditions. In gardens that are very well protected, the growing period is extended considerably. The pruning then can be done earlier.
- Often 2 or 3 buds emerge from the same point on a rose cane. Leaving multiple shoots such as this results in double- or triple-headed canes. Generally, all are weak and subject to splitting under heavy rain or wind stress. It is a good practice to remove all but the largest shoots before they get too big. This can be done by rubbing out those not required.

If you examine a rose cane closely, you will find that every central bud has two side or secondary bud marks. Nature has provided these potential buds to guard against the loss of a primary bud. As a rule these potential buds remain dormant as long as the primary bud is active. Under normal conditions these potential buds do not develop.

Removing Old Blooms — Dead Heading

For stronger and healthier rose bushes that produce larger quantities of blossoms, remove old spent flowers. This is especially important right after the first flush of spring bloom is gone. Removing the spent flowers quickly helps plants produce new canes and blooms immediately.

The removal of dead blooms should be carried out with the same care and attention as basic pruning and cutting for display. Cut to a bud, which means just ¼ inch (6 mm) above a leaf that shelters

Poor cuts

too close to bud

bad angle   jagged cut

Proper cuts

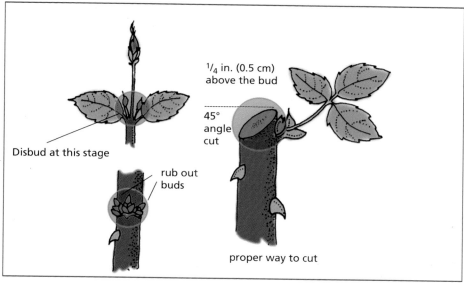

Disbud at this stage

rub out buds

¼ in. (0.5 cm) above the bud

45° angle cut

proper way to cut

Stem pruning

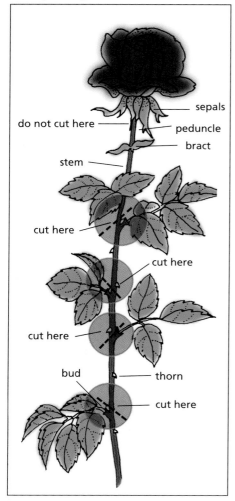

sepals

do not cut here

peduncle

bract

stem

cut here

cut here

cut here

bud

thorn

cut here

Bush pruning

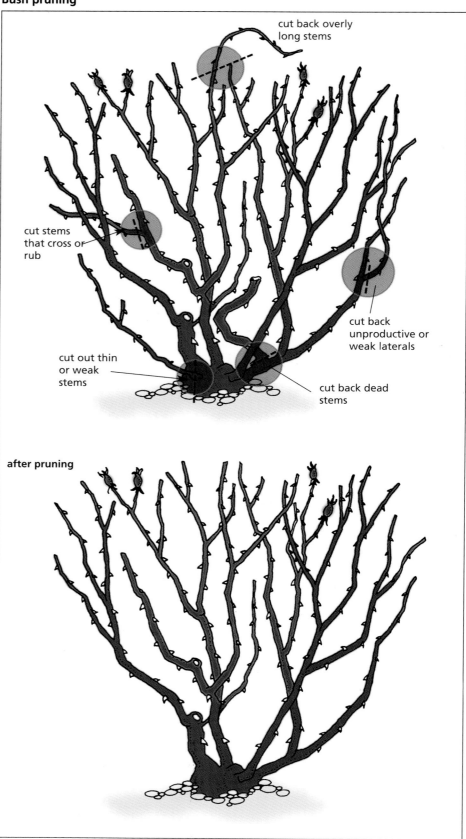

cut back overly
long stems

cut stems
that cross or
rub

cut back
unproductive or
weak laterals

cut out thin
or weak
stems

cut back dead
stems

after pruning

a live bud. Never make a cut halfway between the leaves. Cut dead blooms to the first leaf with a good bud (see illustration). Cut flowers from new bushes with short stems usually back to the first or second leaf. Established roses can be cut back even up to the second leaf from the base if desired. Cut only a few stems this low; leave the rest as long as possible. **It takes at least seven leaves on a cane to manufacture enough food to produce each flower.** That is why leaves should not be removed unnecessarily. The plant needs its leaves. There is an old saying among rose growers that goes like this: 'She loved them to death, cutting every long stem that appeared."

The above comments are not to be confused with cutting for display. For display you want long-stemmed roses with up to seven leaves. For this, care must be exercised not to weaken or kill a bush by cutting out too many long-stemmed flowers.

Cutting Blooms

Very often you have to make tough decisions—do you cut a rose with a long stem and ignore the plant's growth requirements, or do you place the plant's needs first? This is your decision. Do you want to sacrifice future growth or do you want to maintain a healthy plant to produce numerous blooms for several years? The illustration Cutting Rose Blooms illustrates judicious cutting.

Disbudding

Disbudding is a pruning technique that perfectionists and show people practice to obtain a single, large, near-perfect bloom on Hybrid Teas and Grandiflora roses. If you allow the whole set of buds to bloom, you get a lot of color in your garden. Disbudding is done three weeks before a show so that the scars heal prior to presentation.

Blind Wood, Blind Tips

Sometimes a shoot fails to produce a terminal bud. This is termed a "blind end". Where no apparent physical damage is noticeable, it is often due to insect or disease damage. Some cultivars produce more "blind ends", "blind wood", or "blind tips" than others. Some plants do it in early spring and others soon after planting. In a few weeks, blind end plants may start to bloom normally, with shoots originating from side sprouts below the terminal "blind tip". To induce normal growth, cut back a "blind tip" to a good bud immediately. The sooner this is done, the better.

In the rose literature, you may find many theories about "blind wood" but no definitive explanation. In the 1930s, farmers on the plains and prairies were plagued with a similar phenomenon. A normally high yielding variety of oats called "Victory" would occasionally have a large number of aborted florets, called "blossom blast" in those days. This reduced the potentially high yield expected. It was explained by field crop specialists that something happened during its lush growth to reduce critical nutrients. This may have been due to cold, heat, drought, or an actual lack of nutrients in the soil. Rather than having the collapse of the whole plant, nature has provided a partial abandonment of the development of its fruit (flowers). As previously mentioned, in Victory oats it was termed "blossom blast"; in roses it can be called "blind wood", "blind tips", or "blind ends". The following gives credence to this view. On page 70 of Photographic Encyclopedia, 1991, the author, Peter Harkness (a long-time breeder and propagator of roses in England), writes, "Blind shoots – caused by periods of cold or frost in late spring coinciding with the time when the plant would be developing its flower bud cells in inclement weather. Sometimes it is due to lack of nourishment, when the plant does not have the considerable food reserves it needs in order to convert flower buds into blooms." We now have to find how to prevent it. Until answers are found to solve this problem, keep the rose bushes well fed, and diseases and pests under control. Should "blind wood" appear on very small and short canes, they can be ignored or cut off. On heavier canes, the "blind wood" should

Cutting rose blooms

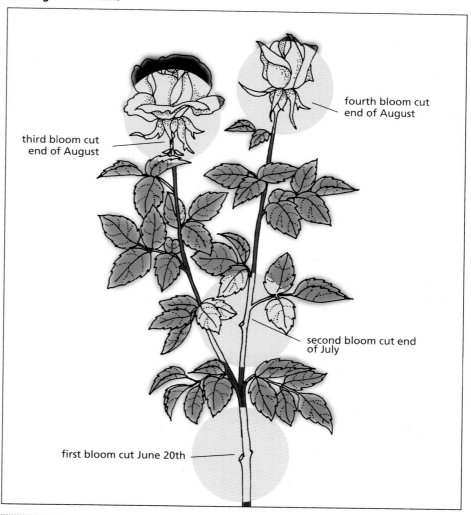

third bloom cut end of August

fourth bloom cut end of August

second bloom cut end of July

first bloom cut June 20th

Normal vs. blind tip

be cut back to a leaf-node or two below (see illustration). The cutting back to a leaf-node stimulates the development of a new bud. If done early enough in the season, the new cane becomes a productive one. If left alone, the "blind tip" remains until fall. The best that can be expected is for the rose to produce a side shoot at a very late date. Quite often it is too late for the production of a bloom.

Correcting blind tips

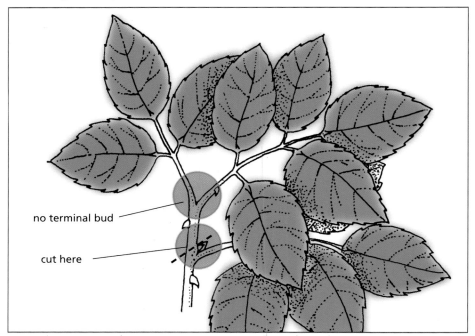

no terminal bud

cut here

How To Keep Rose Bushes Blooming

The basic step for long blooming roses is to use cultivars noted for their florescence and continuity of bloom. Floribundas such as Iceberg, Frensham, Fire King, Europeana, and the Polyantha, The Fairy are noted for this feature. As a rule, Hybrid Tea roses produce fewer flowers per stem than the Floribundas. Even among the Hybrid

Teas there are cultivars that have a greater tendency for repeat blooming than the others. The common popular old cultivars fall into this category. The fact that they have remained popular for so many years is proof enough that they possess this desirable habit.

To ensure a plentiful number of blooms from spring until freeze-up, follow these steps:

- Plant properly and protect the rose bushes as previously recommended.
- Feed according to the recommended schedule.
- Monitor rainfall and, if needed, add supplementary water, making certain that the roses receive at least 1 inch (2.5 cm) per week.
- Control pests.
- Remove old spent flowers quickly.
- Use continuous blooming cultivars.
- Winterize your roses, for annual repeat performance.

Suckers

At times canes with different foliage emerge from the root stock on which the rose is grafted. These are called suckers. Suckers usually have small pale leaves bearing seven or more serrated leaflets, originating from below the graft union. A sucker that is not removed may quickly overtake the upper portion of the plant and completely dominate it. Suckers tend to be tall, vigorous, and unproductive of blossoms.

Quite often a sucker can be pulled up completely without doing much damage to the root system. If pulling is not successful, dig a small hole at the base of the plant. Cut the sucker off flush with the root, as shown in the figure. If any of it is left, it will continue growing.

Staking and Labelling

Tall rose canes growing in unprotected areas may require support to avoid wind damage. Do this by inserting a narrow 3-foot (1-m) stake into the ground near the center of the bush. Tie the more vulnerable canes to the stake using twist-ties. Where the roses have good protection, only the tallest canes may benefit from staking. Young willows make beautiful stakes. Treat the lower 6 inches (15 cm) of the stakes with a wood preservative so they last for several years.

For show purposes, rose stems must be straight. Crooked stems can be straightened by tying the stem to a stake in at least three different places. This should be done about two weeks before the show. Twist-ties are handy for this purpose.

After growing roses for a few years, you will realize that each cultivar has some distinguishing features. Make a point of identifying any cultivar that has impressed you. When Chrysler Imperial is mentioned, you will come to associate that name with a beautifully shaped dark red fragrant rose; when Peace is spoken of, you will think of a large, showy attractive blend of yellow, pink, and white. Label your roses so that the names become familiar to you. Knowing the name of a rose you saw at a flower show or in some garden makes it much easier

to find in gardening catalogues and nurseries.

A purchased rose often has a tag bearing its name wired to one of the canes or container. After planting, remove this tag and fasten it to a stake nearby. Never leave it on the cane because the wire tie can girdle the cane when it starts to grow. Inconspicuous, green or brown stakes and labels are advisable with the rose variety printed on them with a water-proof marker. Naming can also be done with key numbers that refer to a printed list.

Rejuvenating Run-Down Rose Bushes

After a number of years many rose bushes show a "run-down" appearance. If this is allowed to continue, they will eventually not be worth keeping. Rose bushes may show signs of being "run-down" 5 or 6 years after planting. It can be earlier or later, depending largely on the kind of soil and how well it was prepared before planting. One rosarian reported in the *American Rose* magazine,

October 1992 how he had rejuvenated his "run-down" roses. He drills 5 or 6, 2-inch (5-cm) wide holes 10 inches (25 cm) apart, and 12 inches (30 cm) deep around each bush using a variable speed electric drill. The holes are filled with a mixture made up of:

- 16 parts peat moss
- 16 parts perlite
- 4 parts fish emulsion
- 4 parts alfalfa meal
- 2 parts lime
- sulfur depending on the pH of the soil
- 1 part superphosphate.

The author has used this method and can vouch that it improves old, "worn-out" rose bushes.

Another "pick-up" for roses suggested by H. Scott Hansen in the August, 1994 issue of *American Rose* magazine recommends that willow water greatly improves plant growth (willow branches soaked in water for several days contains traces of acetylsalicylic acid). He states that 2 ASA tablets per U.S. gallon (3.8 L) water has the same effect as willow water.

Suckers

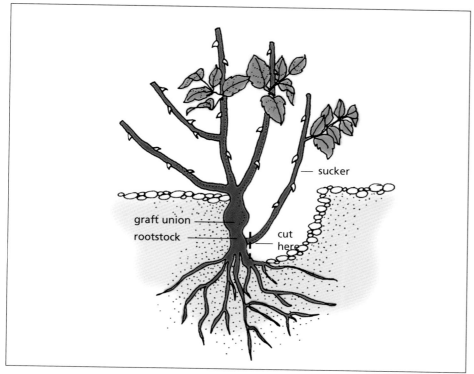

Staking roses

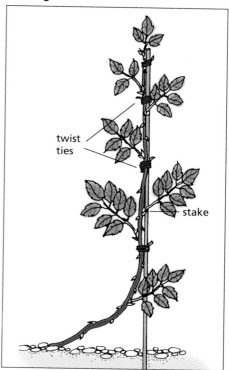

Life Expectancy of a Rose Bush

The life expectancy for the hardy Shrub roses depends on the care they get. With good care they may last a lifetime.

For the tender Hybrid Tea, Grandiflora, Floribunda, and Climbers, various publications report thirty years in some areas. In other areas they are lucky to get five years. In our area (the northern plains and the Canadian prairies) much depends on the rootstock used, the cultivar, and the protection they get. Those that do the best (with the planting method and winter cover recommended in this book) are grafted on *Rosa canina* and *Rosa multiflora* rootstock.

There are rose suppliers who specify the rootstock they use in their propagation. However, many of the roses from American growers are grafted on rootstock that is not hardy in our harsh climate. Those who want their roses to have a longer life span would do well to keep this point in mind. Otherwise, you may as well treat the tender roses as annuals.

Here are some roses in the author's garden considered to be in the old-age group:

Thirty-five years
Lucy Cramphorn

Thirty years
Alaska Centennial, Blanc Double de Coubert, Bonsoir, Comanche, Crimson Glory, Cuthbert Grant, Gail Borden, Ivory Fashion, Mirandy, Miss Canada, Morning Jewel (Climber), My Love, Peace, Pink Parfait, Prairie Dawn, Rose Gaujard, Tropicana

Twenty-five years
Anne Cocker, Ballerina, Dainty Bess, Dortmund, Dr. Brownell, Elizabeth of Glamis, Flamingo Queen, John Waterer, Marie Antoinette, Oriana, Red Queen

There are many in the 10 -to 20-year group. When a rose bush has been productive for four or five years, it owes you nothing. Any number of years beyond that is an excellent dividend.

Growing Roses Organically (using no chemicals)

Many gardeners and rosarians ask how roses can be grown organically, that is, without the use of chemical fertilizers and pesticides. Various sources say that it can be done. Here are some organic rose growing examples:

- Bone meal to supply phosphorous and calcium. All plants and animals require these elements to maintain their growth and health.
- Phosphorous and calcium (lime – used to lower soil pH), both mined, naturally occurring compounds.
- Iron chelates (iron found in soil and rocks) and micronized iron (iron filings) to prevent chlorosis
- Potassium obtained from banana peels, and potassium carbonate (potash) mined from ancient sea beds. This element is required by the plant in the formation of sugars and starches. It helps to keep the plant rigid and stand upright. It also aids the plant to produce materials in cells which can go through frosts without damaging it as water does (anti-freeze).
- Epsom salts – a natural product found on the soil surface in several areas in England and the United States. It is magnesium sulfate. This element composes part of the chlorophyll molecule found in green plant tissues. Chlorophyll is a necessary component in photosynthesis, a process that makes food for the plant. Magnesium also functions to maintain plant health.
- Cow tea, alfalfa tea, alfalfa meal, manure, blood meal, fish meal, liquid fish, and compost which, as they decompose, supply nitrogen and many other elements the plants require.
- Bordeaux mixture is a mix of copper sulfate and calcium hydroxide for the control of blackspot and powdery mildew.
- Household mixture of water, baking soda, and vegetable oil to control powdery mildew.
- Safers Insecticidal Soap (potassium salt) to control insects.
- Natural insecticides with active ingredients naturally or synthetically derived from pyrethrum and derris plants (see your garden center for specific products).
- Water – cold water spray for spider mites.

In some rose publications, you can find how roses may be grown organically with success. Anyone interested in this specialized approach can obtain valuable information from a book titled, *The Encyclopedia of Roses: An Organic Guide to Growing and Enjoying America's Favorite Flower*, published by Rodale Press, Inc., Emmaus, PA 18098, U.S.A.

Pest Control

This section describes the major problem insect, disease, weed, and vertebrate pests found in the northern plains of the United States and prairie provinces of Canada. It is by no means a complete list. Local geographical features, weather variations, microclimate conditions, plus a host of other factors create considerable variability in outbreaks and density of pest infestations across the region on an annual basis. The outstanding characteristics and common control measures of the most consistent problem pests are outlined here.

In the past the recommended strategy for pest control in roses was that of spraying and dusting regularly to prevent insects and diseases from appearing. Today, largely due to environmental and personal safety concerns, this is no longer the recommended approach. Pesticides should be applied only after problems surface and specific pests have been identified. Two or more applications of the recommended pesticide may be necessary to gain control. Most of the pesticides cited in this publication are referred to by their active ingredient, that is, the chemical that actually attacks the identified pest. Numerous pesticide manufactures in various states and provinces have brand or trade names specific to their particular product. In fact, there are so many trade names with the same active ingredient and combinations thereof, no attempt has been made to integrate the trade name alternatives into this book. Find the active ingredient in the tables supplied and seek out a product containing that chemical at your local garden center. The chemicals listed in Tables 42, 43, 45, and 49 are registered for use on roses. You will note that generic pest categories (Caterpillar) are included as well as specific pest categories (Tent caterpillar). This apparent duplication exists due to variations in control and pest data presented by manufacturers when registering their products. It is a wise strategy to aim for the most pest-specific product when selecting pesticides. However, product availability may necessitate making the more generic selection in some cases. Always know your pests, know your pesticides, and read the label before use.

Many pesticides require specialized equipment to safely apply them. Some products are more suitably applied by a licensed applicator. Other chemicals are available that control the various pests cited, but they may not have been tested on rose bushes, or if they have been tested, they may be harmful to the roses in varying degrees or under certain circumstances. **Always read the label before applying any pesticide.**

In addition, pesticides are added to and deleted from registration lists in various jurisdictions periodically. Therefore, use the tables as a guide only, and if you choose to use pesticides in your garden, keep up-to-date on the subject.

In the continental United States, 122 insect pests have been shown to infest roses, including various species of the following:

Insect	No. of Species
aphids	8
bees	2
beetles	15
borers	5
bugs	3
caterillars	11
leaf hoppers	6
leaf rollers	4
mites	5
moths	2
sawfly	4
scale	25
thrips	6
weavils	4
worms	6

This table illustrates the scope and variation of the potential insect problem. The same applies to diseases, weeds, and vertebrate pests. The pests you experience may go well beyond those specifically highlighted in this book. The tables provide you with some additional information. Study your pests, and read the label before applying pesticides.

Insects

Many common garden insect pests love roses. The most prevalent include:
- aphids (Homoptera: Aphididae)
- caterpillars (Lepidoptera)
- leaf-cutter bees (Hymenoptera: Megachilidae)
- leafhoppers (Homoptera: Cicadellidae)
- midge (Diptera)
- minute pirate bugs (Hemiptera: Anthocoridae)
- pear slugs (Hymenoptera: Symphyta, Tenthredinidae *Caliroa cerasi* (Linnaeus))
- rose curculio (weevil) (Caleoptera Curcalionidae *Rhyncites bicolor* (Fabricius))
- slugs (Mollusca Limacidae Limax)
- spider mites (Acarina: Tetranychidae)
- tarnished plant bugs (Hemiptera: Miridae *Lygus lineolaris* (Palisot de Beauvois))
- thrips (Thysanoptera)

Aphids

Aphids are slow moving, soft bodied, winged or wingless, pear-shaped insects up to ⅛ inch (3 mm) long. They suck plant juices from the tender terminal shoots and buds, and seek cover underneath the foliage. Aphids excrete a sticky, shiny, honey-dew substance that will be readily noticeable in a sizeable infestation.

Aphids appear throughout the growing season in green or dark brown clusters that take on a black appearance in late August and September. Plants lose

Aphid

Caterpillar

Alberta Agriculture, Food and Rural Development

Caterpillar damage

Alberta Agriculture, Food and Rural Development

vigor and are sometimes stunted; the leaves show yellowing, curling, or puckering; and the flowers and buds become deformed. The honeydew they excrete attracts ants and carriers of bacterial, fungal, and viral diseases. Black sooty molds may grow on the honeydew. Generally, aphids are easy to control by simply spraying insecticidal soap.

Caterpillars

Caterpillars are the larvae of various butterflies and moths. Perhaps the most damaging are the Forest Tent Caterpillars and the fluffy, black and yellow striped, Woolybear Caterpillars.

Ordinarily caterpillars feed on the native Trembling Aspen (White Poplar), willows, and fruit trees. However, because of their voracious appetite, they quickly defoliate their original host trees and shrubs, and move to adjacent food sources. They love roses, too, and in their migration can quickly consume the rose foliage and blossoms if left unchecked.

Most of the common insecticides effectively control caterpillars. The problem of treatment arises when the caterpillars migrate. Controlling caterpillars on trees and shrubs in the vicinity will reduce the infestation in the rose garden.

Leaf-cutter Bees

The leaf-cutter bee looks like a half sized hornet. These insects are very shy, and they do their leaf-cutting job quickly.

The damage done by these insects is easily detectable by the circular shaped notches cut out of the rose leaflets. The insect uses these pieces of rose leaves to line and patch up the wood tunnels they make for rearing their young.

To deter them from landing on your roses, use a rose dust or insecticidal soap. Leaf-cutter bees are very sensitive to foreign substances on rose foliage and will, as a rule, avoid foliage with any pesticide residue on it.

Leafhoppers

Leafhoppers are ⅛ to ¼ inch (3 to 6 mm) long, wedge shaped, greenish yellow, whitish, or grey. Some are spotted or banded. They suck from the underside of

leaves and hop away when disturbed. Leafhoppers carry and spread many plant diseases, especially viruses. Several broods are produced each year.

Plants infested by leafhoppers look stippled, stunted, lack vigor, and lose color. The leaves become crinkled and curled, and may show white dots or blotches. The underside of leaves show dark specks of excrement.

Most garden insecticides will control this pest.

Midge

This tiny insect damages the newly emerging rose buds causing them to wither, blacken, and die. The midge lays its eggs on the tips (especially on the newly formed flower buds). The eggs hatch in two or three days – the larvae feed on the bud stems or tips – mature and drop into the soil where they, in a

Leafhopper

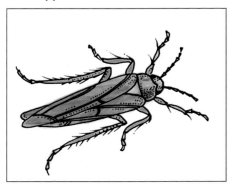

Leaf-cutter bee

Minute pirate bug

Pear slug

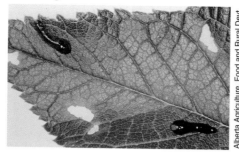

Alberta Agriculture, Food and Rural Devt.

Rose curculio

short time, go through several stages of metamorphosis, become adults, and emerge to lay more eggs. There are several generations in a growing season.

When this pest first appears, use a granular or liquid formation of diazinon as a soil treatment, or spray foliage, particularly on the terminal tips, with a recommended insecticide as a follow-up treatment.

Many rosarians claim that the midge can be responsible for blind ends. In the author's experience, most blind ends are not insect related.

Minute Pirate Bugs or Flower Bugs

These insects are black with white markings, and very small, ⅛ inch (3 mm) long. Their wings fold flat over the abdomen. They have piercing, sucking mouth parts. The young (nymphs) resemble the adults except for their smaller size and the absence of wings. The antenna are about ¼ the length of the body.

These bugs are found on a variety of flowers or under loose bark and in leaf litter. Although they are generally known as predators on other insects and their eggs, they do exercise their piercing mouths on the tender terminal growth and flower buds of roses. They have also been reported to occasionally bite humans. The result is worse than a mosquito sting and more like a black fly bite. Damage done by these insects appears in the form of deformed leaves, spots on leaves, blackened terminal shoots, drooping buds that die, blasted buds, damaged flower bud tops, and imperfect flowers.

Pear Slugs

Pear slugs look like miniature garden slugs, with the head end thicker than the body. They are dark and slimy, and about ¼ inch (6 mm) long when mature. Usually two generations of pear slugs are produced in a year.

These insects skim off the top leaf layer and leave behind the lower epidermis of the leaf which looks like a transparent membrane. Large populations of pear slugs can readily defoliate a rose bush.

Rose Curculio (Weevil)

The insect is a ⅓ inch (8 mm) long, reddish brown to black, hard-bodied, long nosed weevil. It moves slowly, plays dead, and falls to the ground when disturbed. When you find rose buds pierced through their sides, you know this beetle is around, whether you see it

Weevil damage

or not. The bud is probed with the beetle's proboscis in search of rose juice. Perforated buds wilt and dry or fail to open.

Slugs

Slugs may be grey, orange, or black, and vary in size from 1 to 4 inches (2.5 to 10 cm) in length. Their movement is very slow and they leave behind silvery, slimy trails. During the day they hide out under debris or litter of some kind in a dark, damp location. They come out of hiding at night or during damp, cloudy weather to feed.

They feed on and damage the foliage of most garden plants. Slugs are particularly plentiful and can cause much damage in wet years.

Active ingredients registered for insect control on roses

Insect	allethrin	carbaryl	diazinon	d-phenothrin	d-trans allethrin	dicofol	dimethoate	lime sulphur or calcium polysulphide	malathion	methoxychlor	mineral oil (insecticidal or adjuvant)	n-octyl bicycloheptene dicarboximide	oxydemeton-methyl	permethrin	phosmet	piperonyl butoxide	pirimicarb	pyrethrins	resmethrin	rotenone	safer's insecticidal soap	silicon dioxide salt water fossils	soap	sulphur	tetramethrin plus related compounds
ant			✓																						
aphid	✓	✓	✓	✓	✓	✓	✓		✓	✓		✓	✓	✓		✓	✓	✓	✓	✓	✓	✓	✓	✓	✓
armyworm (larvae)					✓								✓			✓									
armyworm		✓			✓	✓							✓	✓		✓		✓							
beetle		✓							✓	✓						✓		✓		✓					
birch leafminer		✓																							
black scale								✓			✓														
blister beetle		✓														✓		✓							
brown soft scale																✓		✓				✓		✓	
bud moth									✓																
bug		✓														✓		✓		✓					
cankerworm		✓							✓	✓										✓				✓	
caterpillar	✓	✓	✓	✓	✓	✓			✓	✓		✓	✓	✓		✓	✓	✓		✓				✓	✓
chewing insect					✓				✓	✓		✓				✓		✓		✓					
chinch bug			✓																						
curculio									✓																
climbing cutworm		✓			✓								✓			✓		✓							
codling moth									✓	✓														✓	
cucumber beetle		✓			✓								✓			✓		✓							
cutworm			✓																						
diamondback moth (larvae)																✓		✓							
earwig		✓				✓							✓								✓		✓		
eastern tent caterpillar				✓									✓			✓									
flea beetle		✓	✓		✓				✓	✓			✓			✓	✓	✓		✓				✓	
flower thrips																✓		✓							
fruit fly			✓																						
fruitworm									✓											✓					
gnat																✓	✓								
grasshopper		✓				✓			✓				✓												
green fruitworm									✓	✓														✓	
gypsy moth		✓												✓		✓		✓							
harlequin bug																✓		✓							
insect (egg)								✓			✓														
insect (egg – overwintering)								✓			✓														
insect		✓	✓	✓					✓	✓	✓	✓				✓		✓						✓	
japanese beetle	✓	✓		✓	✓				✓				✓		✓	✓	✓	✓	✓					✓	✓
june beetle		✓																							
lace bug		✓		✓	✓				✓	✓			✓			✓	✓	✓		✓				✓	✓

Active ingredients registered for insect control on roses (continued)

Insect	allethrin	carbaryl	diazinon	d-phenothrin	d-trans allethrin	dicofol	dimethoate	lime sulphur or calcium polysulphide	malathion	methoxychlor	mineral oil (insecticidal or adjuvant)	n-octyl bicycloheptene dicarboximide	oxydemeton-methyl	permethrin	phosmet	piperonyl butoxide	pirimicarb	pyrethrins	resmethrin	rotenone	safer's insecticidal soap	silicon dioxide salt water fossils	soap	sulphur	tetramethrin plus related compounds
leafhopper	✓	✓	✓	✓	✓	✓	✓		✓	✓		✓	✓	✓		✓	✓	✓	✓	✓				✓	✓
leafminer		✓	✓			✓			✓				✓			✓		✓		✓				✓	
leafroller		✓			✓				✓	✓	✓		✓			✓	✓	✓		✓				✓	
leaftier																✓		✓							
leatherjacket		✓																							
looper		✓							✓	✓						✓		✓							
meadow spittlebug		✓				✓							✓												
mealybug		✓	✓	✓	✓				✓			✓	✓			✓					✓		✓	✓	
mite		✓	✓	✓	✓	✓	✓		✓	✓			✓			✓	✓	✓	✓	✓				✓	✓
moth																✓		✓							
plant bug		✓				✓			✓	✓			✓				✓		✓						
poplar-and-willow leaf beetle		✓																							
psyllid		✓				✓							✓								✓			✓	
root maggot			✓																						
root weevil			✓																						
rose aphid		✓							✓																
rose chafer		✓	✓			✓			✓	✓			✓			✓	✓	✓		✓			✓	✓	✓
rose leaf beetle										✓								✓						✓	
rose leafhopper		✓							✓	✓								✓				✓	✓	✓	✓
rose scale								✓			✓														
rose slug		✓							✓	✓						✓	✓	✓		✓			✓	✓	
rust mite		✓			✓								✓												
sawfly (larvae)		✓				✓			✓	✓			✓											✓	✓
sawfly		✓							✓							✓	✓	✓		✓		✓			
scale		✓	✓			✓		✓	✓		✓		✓			✓	✓	✓							
spider mite	✓	✓	✓	✓	✓	✓			✓	✓	✓	✓	✓			✓		✓		✓			✓	✓	✓
spittlebug																		✓							
stink bug																✓		✓							
subterranean cutworm			✓																						
sucking insect				✓	✓							✓				✓		✓							✓
tarnished plant bug		✓							✓	✓						✓		✓							
tent caterpillar		✓		✓					✓	✓						✓		✓						✓	
thrips	✓	✓	✓		✓	✓	✓		✓	✓		✓	✓	✓		✓	✓	✓	✓	✓				✓	
twospotted spider mite													✓			✓		✓	✓						✓
webworm																✓		✓							
weevil										✓															
whitefly		✓		✓	✓				✓	✓		✓	✓			✓	✓	✓	✓	✓				✓	✓

Slug

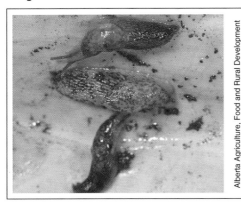

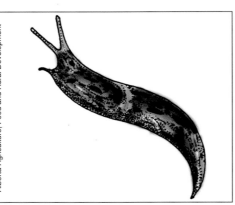

Alberta Agriculture, Food and Rural Development

Slug bait station

Spider mite

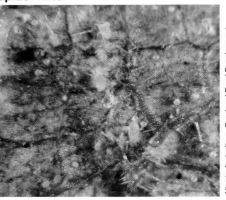

Alberta Agriculture, Food and Rural Development

Control of slugs is somewhat different and more difficult than for most insects. Insecticides commonly used for other insects are ineffective for slugs. Some gardeners resort to table salt (sodium chloride) and lime. This will kill slugs, but there is the danger that several applications each year and continued use of the mixture will seriously affect the quality and productivity of the soil. A more effective and safer method would be treatment with a slug bait containing metaldehyde that is placed in protected bait or feeding stations. The stations are placed in shaded areas under the sheltering foliage of large plants and shrubs. These cafeteria type self-feeders may be purchased at garden centers.

Feeding stations may be made by using a coffee jar lid and an empty plastic honey or margarine container. The jar lid should be a bit smaller in diameter than the plastic container. The jar lid serves as a dish to hold the poison bait and the inverted plastic container provides the shelter to keep the bait dry and the location shady. Attach three popsicle sticks (evenly spaced) to the inside of the plastic container, and allow the sticks to protrude. Krazy Glue works well for attaching the sticks to the plastic container. Stick the legs of this container into the soil over the dish of bait allowing about ¾ inch (2 cm) of crawl space. Inspect, clean, and renew the poison bait every two or three days. The anchored container stays "put" in rain and wind. It

also prevents birds and small pets from picking up the poison bait. **Note:** Be very careful if there is any possibility of children being about. Additional safeguards must also be considered for cats and dogs, as metaldehyde is deadly to these species.

A general clean-up, along with chemical use, is necessary to obtain good control. A favorite shelter of slugs is tall un-cut grass, under board sidewalks, in woodpiles, and under debris lying on the ground. Removal of litter and mowing tall grass and weeds leaves them without adequate shelter.

Spider Mites

Spider mites are not really insects. They are related to spiders, ticks, and scorpions, but for convenience most people group them with insects. Spider mites may be brown, green, yellow, red, or black, and are oval shaped and wingless. They are slow moving and less than ¹⁄₁₆ inch (1 mm) in length. They feed by sucking sap and are usually found on the underside of the leaves. Spider mites reproduce rapidly, especially under dry, sunny conditions, and may produce many generations a year.

Very fine silky cobwebs on the underside of leaves, in the leaf axis, and sometimes covering the whole shoot are indications of spider mite infestation. The hard-to-see spider mites can sometimes be easily detected by tapping leaves over a piece of white paper. When

severely infested, leaves show pale spots on the upper side, appear mottled, speckled, or dusty, and will eventually turn yellow or brown and fall off.

Spider mites are the most persistent and perhaps the most difficult insect pest to control in the rose garden. Because spider mites abhor rain and damp conditions, perhaps the safest and most economical method of controlling this pest is to spray the underside of the leaves with cold water. Spraying two days apart for three or four repetitions usually controls this pest.

People who are averse to the use of chemicals use this method to control them. Each week they spray the rose bushes with water being certain to wet the underside of the foliage. This manages to ward off spider mite damage, but it must be practiced religiously whenever spider mites or their damage is sighted.

Active ingredients registered for insect control on greenhouse roses

Greenhouse Insect	allethrin	carbaryl	diazinon	d-phenothrin	d-trans allethrin	dicofol	dimethoate	lime sulphur or calcium polysulphide	malathion	methoxychlor	mineral oil (insecticidal or adjuvant)	n-octyl bicycloheptene dicarboximide	oxydemeton-methyl	permethrin	phosmet	piperonyl butoxide	pirimicarb	pyrethrins	resmethrin	rotenone	safer's insecticidal soap	silicon dioxide salt water fossils	soap	sulphur	tetramethrin plus related compounds
aphid																✓		✓	✓						✓
blister beetle																✓		✓							
diamondback moth (larvae)																✓		✓							
flea beetle																✓		✓							
harlequin bug																✓		✓							
leafhopper																✓		✓							
leaftier																✓		✓							
looper																✓		✓							
rose chafer																✓		✓							
roseslug																✓		✓							
spider mite																✓		✓							
stink bug																✓		✓							
tarnished plant bug																✓		✓							
two spotted spider mite																			✓						✓
webworm																✓		✓							
whitefly																✓		✓	✓						✓

Spider mite damage

Repeated applications of a malathion, diazinon, or dimethoate solution is also quite effective in spider mite control. Chemicals made specifically for spider mite control are cited in the table on page 43.

"Avid", released in 1987 for horticultural use in the United States, is reported in the American Rose Magazine and Rose Ramblings Bulletin of the Spokane Rose Society to be the most effective chemical to date for the control of spider mites. "Avid" kills the adults and the eggs. The recommendation is to spray twice, one week apart, just to make certain that all spider mites and eggs are killed.

Tarnished plant bug

Alberta Agriculture, Food and Rural Development

Tarnished Plant Bugs

The mature bugs are ⅓ inch (8 mm) long, and are flattish and oval shaped. They are mottled with yellow, white, and black, and have a yellow triangle on the lower third of each side. Young bugs (nymphs) are under ¼ inch (6 mm), and greenish yellow, with five black dots. They are very shy and move very fast. Adults quickly fly away when approached. There are one or two broods a season. Adults hibernate in weeds and trash in fall.

Damage done by these insects is similar to that of Minute Pirate Bugs.

Thrips

This tiny insect is up to ¹⁄₂₀ of an inch (under 1 mm) in length and about half the thickness of the letter "i" in this text. Its two pairs of wings are two-thirds the length of the whole body, feathery and folded up neatly over the body when not in flight. Its flight is fast and movement on plants is quick and agile. It has a rasping sucking mouthpart. The insect is

Thrip

difficult to see because of its minute size and fast movement. When disturbed, it prefers to fly rather than crawl. It is easiest to find and see by briskly tapping an infested blossom on your palm or a piece of white paper, and using a magnifying glass. Thrip droppings are black and shiny and the deposit is a good indication of the insects' presence. Many broods are produced each year.

Tiny translucent spots on rose petals, especially noticeable on clear white or very dark petals, are often formed by the minute thrips. They probe and suck the delicious rose petal juice. (This is very similar to a mosquito or flea sucking your blood.) A large number of these spots on petals renders a rose bloom useless for show purposes. Swarms of thrips can cause rose buds to fail to open.

Thrips, although they are considered easy to kill, are difficult to control. Although they can be killed by almost any insecticide, they get inside flowers and buds where ordinarily insecticides do not get to them. Thrips also reproduce in profusion, feeding on a great variety of plants, and flying about invading newer and better locations. Here is where the use of a systemic insecticide, such as dimethoate, may be necessary. The chemical enters the plant, so that it becomes lethal to feeding insects. Another advantage is that it remains toxic for a week or longer, depending on the weather.

See the tables on pages 42, 43 and 45 for pest control products registered for control of specific insects on roses.

Diseases

It has been said, "Almost anyone can grow roses in the spring. It is the summer, fall, and winter that separates the successes from the failures." If you have reached mid-August and have had very few problems with insects and damage from disease, you are headed for success. The care given your roses from mid-August on ensures good growth and health the following year.

General Control of Rose Diseases

A thorough clean-up of leaves and other debris reduces the places that insects and fungi can overwinter. If you are experiencing disease problems, spray the canes and the soil around rose bushes with a fungicide after the cleanup.

Most fungal diseases thrive under warm, humid conditions. Therefore, avoid the use of overhead sprinklers in the evening, which would permit the roses to remain damp overnight. When overhead sprinklers are used, do the watering early in the morning as this should enable the foliage to dry off during the day and reduce the prolonged moist condition that encourages some disease problems.

For an expanded list of fungicides registered for use on roses, see page 49. Of the different fungicides available, clear liquid solutions are preferable to dusts because they do not leave unsightly residues on the flowers and foliage.

Black Spot (*Diplocarpon rosae*)

Black spot first appears on the upper surface of the lower leaves of a rose bush as round black spots up to ½ inch (12 mm) in diameter. The spots are often surrounded by a yellow halo. The leaves will soon yellow and drop off. The Shrub rose, Persian Yellow, is very susceptible. Others vary from mildly susceptible to resistant to this disease.

Black spot fungus spores over-winter on dead leaves or canes, and are spread by spores splashing up from the soil during watering or rainfall. If the fungus enters the leaf, its progress cannot be halted without destroying the leaf. An infected plant may lose all its leaves, then put out new ones, lose those and start leafing a third time. This drastically weakens the plant to the point where it may not survive the winter.

A black spot prevention program includes a thorough clean-up in the fall. All diseased leaves should be raked up and destroyed throughout the growing season. Diseased canes should be pruned off and cut back several inches into good wood.

Black spot

The *Rose Hybridizers Newsletter*, winter 1985, offers a non-toxic black spot control from W.R. Shaw of Sydney, Australia. He sprays weekly with baking soda, using 2 tbsp. in 5 quarts (6 mL in 1 L) of water mixed with a spreader sticker. Shaw describes the formula as effective against both black spot and mildew. Shaw also uses, on occasion, a weekly spray of Lysol as a cure and preventative for mildew, mixed at the rate of 1 oz. in 5 quarts (6 mL in 1 L) of water.

Black Spot Free Roses

Over the next few years, a great variety of roses resistant to black spot will appear on the market. In 1979, a U.S.D.A. research scientist, Peter Semeniuk, developed three Hybrid Tea roses – Spotless Pink, Spotless Gold, and Spotless Yellow. The research administration has released budding material from these cultivars to amateur and commercial rose breeders in the United States.

Because there are over fifty different strains of black spot, it is difficult for plant breeders to develop resistant cultivars.

Botrytis Blight (*Botrytis cinerea*)

This fungus disease mainly attacks Hybrid Tea roses. Leaves and canes are attacked, revealing a grayish, black-to-brown fuzzy lesion. The flower buds brown, droop, fail to open, and eventually decay.

Botrytis blight lives on dying plant tissue and, when conditions are right, can release thousands of spores. Infection generally occurs when water remains on leaves and buds of stressed plants.

To control the disease, cut and destroy all infected buds, leaves, and canes. A fungicide application may be required to gain control.

Brown Canker (*Cryptosporella umbrina*)

This fungal disease is capable of attacking any portion of the rose above ground and can result in the death of the entire stem.

The disease first appears as small red to purple spots on the current year's canes, then develops into gray-white lesions on the entire stem. Usually by the second year, the lesions enlarge into brown cankers several inches long. Girding of the stem produces death. If the cankers extend down to the crown, they may destroy the entire plant.

Crown gall

Although the fungus is spread by splashing water, wind, and pruning tools, the pathogen can only enter the plant through wounds.

To prevent the disease, select disease-free planting stock. Once established, prune out and destroy all diseased canes. Make cuts well below the infected area, and before each cut, dip the pruning shears into a one-part chlorine bleach to eight-parts water solution.

Crown Gall (*Agrobacterium tumefaciens*)

This bacterial disease appears as rough, roundish, tumor-like growths on rose canes near soil level. Infected plants lose vigor, become stunted, and eventually die. The galls contain numerous bacteria which can spread to other roses. Crown gall bacteria gain entry to plants through bruises and injury.

Here is what many rose growers do to control this disease:
- Cyril C. Harris, in his book, "Beginners Guide to Rose Growing", recommends cutting away infected parts and painting with Bacticin (published by Sphere Books Ltd., London).

- James Underwood Crockett (Time-Life Books, New York) in his book "Roses", recommends removal of galls and spraying with streptomycin which may be obtained in spray or powder form at garden stores.
- Many gardeners have reported in the American Rose Society and Spokane Rose Society monthly magazines that they have successfully used common household disinfectants such as Lysol, household bleach, and rubbing alcohol. The galls are removed and the wound painted with the disinfectant. Cutting tools are also treated to prevent the spread of bacteria.
- A 1998 innovation is agrobacterium radiobacter, strain 84. It provides biological control when used as a soil drench or by dipping the roots into the solution before planting. This product is available under the trade name of Galltrol-A, and also from another supplier as Gallex (curative) or Galltrol (biological preventative).
- Before planting a new rose in infected soil, dig out a hole and discard the soil. Remove and replace a volume of soil up to three times that of the root ball from the area of the infected plant. Spray the hole and surrounding area with a solution of copper fungicide. Dip the roots in a copper fungicide solution, and plant the rose using new, clean soil. Roses should not be planted in crown gall infected soil for at least five years.
- Sodium methyldithio-carbamate can also be used to disinfect crown gall infested soil. It is not safe to use this product around live plants. You may need a certified pesticide applicator to use this product in some jurisdictions.
- Dig up and burn the diseased rose bush.
- Prevent water logging by providing adequate drainage. Crown Gall is rarely seen in roses grown in well drained, porous type soils.
- Avoid injury to the rose bush at or near the soil surface when cultivating.

Powdery mildew

Downy or Black Mildew
(*Peronospora sparsa*)

Downy or Black Mildew is not commonly a great problem on the plains and prairies, although it does present problems under certain circumstances. It is likely to occur in protected areas when the temperature is about 70°F (21°C), in high humidity, or where roses are grown in greenhouses.

In infected plants, the upper surfaces of the leaves show irregular brown or brownish-purple spots and shrivel. The underside shows gray tufts. In severe infections, the leaves fall off easily.

Infection can be prevented by spraying with maneb or another recommended product every 9 to 10 days (see table opposite).

Powdery Mildew
(*Sphaerotheca pannosa*)

Powdery mildew is most common in the humid rose-growing areas of the United States and Canada. In the northern plains of the United States and Canada it does not generally present a

major problem except when the fall is cool and damp. At this late stage it rarely does any serious damage to roses. It is a fungal disease appearing as grayish or white patches on tender rose parts including the buds. The patches resemble a layer of felt which contain thousands of fungal spores and give the plant a frosty, powdery appearance. The leaves become stunted, thickened, and distorted. Stems are also stunted and the buds fail to open.

Powdery mildew grows on the surface of both sides of leaves and invades the plant deeply. It is prolonged damp or warm humid conditions that promote the growth of powdery mildew. Cloudy days, moist nights, and poor air circulation are very conducive to the growth and spread of the disease. Late afternoon watering can contribute to this disease developing. Ideally, watering should be completed very early in the morning so the foliage dries off quickly.

Good management practices will help prevent this disease. Destroy all diseased leaves and canes throughout the growing season. Many fungicides are commonly used to control Powdery Mildew (see table opposite).

Another recipe for powdery mildew control appeared in the magazine *The American Rose*, September 1992. " Spray once a week with a solution made of 3 tsp. baking soda, 1 gallon (3.8 L) warm water, 1½ tsp. dishwashing detergent (not the machine dishwashing type), 2½ tbsp. vegetable oil. " The author has used it with good results on roses and begonias.

Rust (*Phragmidium species*)

Nine species of rust fungus are found on roses. There is a high degree of cultivar variability in resistance to the disease. Rose rust first appears as small yellow pinprick marks on the upper surface of leaves low on a plant. Later, clusters of orange or black pustules appear on the underside of the leaf. Spores from these pustules are blown to

Rust

other leaves and start new infections. Under cool, humid conditions these pustules may infect and eventually defoliate the bush. In early fall the pustules change color and become black. These overwinter in the leaf tissue to produce spores the following spring.

An integrated management program can maintain control of rust:
- Use resistant varieties
- Maintain good sanitation – keep the garden clean.
- Apply fungicide when necessary (see table).

Viral Diseases

Like most plants, roses are sometimes afflicted with various viral infections. They are spread mostly by biting and sucking insects, or by garden tools such as the hoe, cultivator, or pruner. There are no chemical controls for viral diseases. Control is largely a matter of prevention. Nursery operators know this and strive to develop and maintain disease-free stock for their cuttings and bud-wood. Fortunately in Canada and the United States to date there have been no major problems with viral diseases in roses. If viral problems are suspected, they should be properly identified (state and provincial governments, universities, or private plant pathologists usually offer this service).

Active ingredients registered for disease control on roses

Diseases	Active Ingredients											
	benomyl	captan	copper as elemental*	copper as elemental**	dichlone	folpet	lime sulphur or calcium polysulfide	maneb	sulphur	thiophanate-methyl	triforine	zineb
black spot	✓	✓		✓	✓	✓	✓	✓	✓	✓	✓	✓
blight		✓										
botrytis leaf spot						✓			✓			✓
canker								✓				
downy mildew				✓					✓			
leaf spot		✓		✓					✓			✓
mildew		✓						✓	✓			
petal blight									✓			✓
powdery mildew	✓	✓		✓	✓	✓			✓	✓	✓	✓
rose canker								✓				
rose rust									✓			
rust				✓					✓			✓
scab									✓			
stem rot						✓						

* present as copper oxychloride
** present as tribasic copper sulphate

Rose Mosaic

Another common world-wide virus is the rose mosaic. It does not appear to hinder the plant's growth. When this virus becomes established, intricate yellow patterns are formed on the foliage.

Most commercial rose propagators now cure Rose Mosaic by subjecting their plants to a special heat treatment technique. In the future this disease may become very rare unless new strains develop an immunity to this treatment.

Rose mosaic

Rose Wilt

A common viral disease in some countries is rose wilt. The whole plant or just a shoot may collapse and die. To prevent the spread of this disease, the entire plant or at least the infected portion should be removed and burned.

Do not let insect pest or disease control problems deter you from the fun of growing roses. It is not as formidable a task as some would have you believe. Exercising caution and using common sense with chemicals will get you safely through this necessary task. Reading labels and wearing protective equipment are essential when you apply pesticides.

Weeds

When you are fighting an enemy and expect to win, you must learn all about the enemy. You have to understand the enemy's weak points, and how and when to attack, otherwise you'll be the loser.

Chemical Weed Control

Home or hobby gardeners who do not produce commercially need to recognize that chemical weed control in areas other than lawns is generally not recommended. Chemical weed control is a complex operation in small areas in the vicinity of sensitive plants. A hobby gardener may not have proper equipment and will often find it difficult to apply the correct rate of herbicide on a small scale. Individuals who know how to use herbicides make a point of keeping up-to-date on the numerous weed control chemicals and their uses. In garden weed control, chemicals must be used with extreme caution.

In spite of the cautions already stated, there are chemicals that can be used very effectively for controlling certain weeds in certain circumstances (see page 55). Such cases include the following:

- If you wish to establish a rose garden in an area infested with Canada thistle, quack grass, or other persistent perennials, you can do so

Spraying in Hot Weather

Do not spray liquid insecticides or fungicides when temperatures are higher than 72°F (22°C) or there will be spotting and burning of foliage and blossoms. If you must control insects or diseases during high temperatures, use a dust. This will not burn the foliage.

with glyphosate. Glyphosate is also available in numerous ready to spray products handled by your local garden center. Used according to instructions on the label, this product will eliminate weeds and render the soil suitable for cultivation and growing roses in about ten days. The weeds must be actively growing at the time of chemical application.

- Perennial weeds growing in the rose bed may be treated individually by painting their foliage with a prepared solution of glyphosate using a small paint brush. **Do not get the chemical on either the leaves or bark of the rose bushes.**

Cultural Weed Control

Most rose gardeners rely on cultural weed control methods that include mulching, hoeing, cultivating, and hand weeding.

Mulch may be any organic material such as decomposed manure, peat moss, compost, chopped weed-free straw or hay, or lawn clippings if free from herbicides. A mulch about 2 to 3 inches (5 to 8 cm) thick will retard weed growth, conserve moisture, and maintain a uniform soil temperature. In time, the mulch decomposes and becomes part of the soil organic matter thereby enriching the garden soil.

All weeds can be controlled by covering them with heavy cardboard, black plastic, or many layers of newspaper. These are kept in place by laying small scoopfuls of soil on the edges over the cover. The cover should be light

in weight and sun-proof. Any hole or inadequate covering will allow light to enter and keep the weeds alive. In a month or so the weeds will succumb. One problem is that it does not eliminate the weeds that get into the center of the bush or the seeds in the soil. In addition, it gives an untidy look to the garden.

To keep ahead of the weeds, hoe or cultivate when the weeds are under 2 inches (5 cm), and the soil surface is dry. Frequent hoeings are much easier and effective than wrestling tough, large weeds from the soil. Cultivation should be shallow so that the roots of the roses are not damaged.

Weeds that are freshly germinated, and 1 to 2 inches (2 to 4 cm) can be smothered by laying and anchoring a sheet of black plastic over the area. In 2 to 3 weeks in spring and summer, the weeds and roots will be dead.

Knowing the salient features of problem weeds will help you control them. A starting point in understanding weed control is recognizing the various life cycles of the problem weeds, and capitalizing on the opportunities this presents. This is true of either chemical or cultural weed control practices. The problem weeds listed later are categorized according to life cycle.

Annuals complete their life cycle in a single growing season. Seedlings that start too late to mature seed are killed by frost in the fall.

Biennials or winter annuals do not usually produce seed in their first growing year, but have the ability to overwinter and then continue their growth the following year to mature and produce seed. If weather conditions permit, however, winter annuals may mature and produce seed in a single year.

Perennials are plants that can generate growth from seed or root stock. They are capable of seed production, overwintering, and continued growth, and spread for many years.

Annuals

Annual Poa
Poa annua

This is a short-lived annual grassy weed. It is related to other perennial blue grasses except that its leaves are pale green and very soft. It grows in clumps that are easy to pull. It is a prolific seed producer, which makes it a nuisance in the home garden. It germinates at any time during the summer especially when the soil is damp. This habit makes it tough to eradicate. This grass does not survive the winter.

Common Groundsel
Senecio vulgaris

The stems are hollow, usually branched, and 6 to 16 inches (15 to 40 cm) high; leaves are lobed and toothed. Flowers come in clusters at the end of the branches. They are ¼ inch (6 mm) across and yellow. The small seeds are attached to a fluffy fuzz which permits them to be easily carried by the wind. The seeds germinate at any time during the summer making them a constant pest in the garden. Mature plants are difficult to pull and most often break off just above ground level.

Common groundsel

Alberta Agriculture, Food, and Rural Development

Corn Spurry (also known as devil's-gut, sandweed, pickpurse)
Spergula arvensis

This plant grows with several stems, 6 to 18 inches (15 to 45 cm) high, forming at the base. The stems are a little hairy and sticky. Leaves are very narrow, 1 to 2 inches (2.5 to 5 cm) long, and curving upward in clusters. Flowers are white, about ¼ inch (6 mm) across, and attached to the top of the stems by thin stalks. It is a prolific seed producer with seeds germinating at any time during the summer.

Flixweed

Alberta Agriculture, Food, and Rural Development

Flixweed
Descuroinia sophia

This annual and sometimes biennial is gray-green in color due to tiny branched hairs, and up to 3 feet (1 m) in height. The leaves are up to 4 inches (10 cm) long, alternate, and divided 2 to 3 times into narrow leaflets. Flowering throughout the summer, the pale yellow blossoms are very small, and clustered at the top of the stem, with petals as long as or shorter than the sepals. The seeds are contained in slender, slightly curved pods about ¾ inch (2 cm) long. The seeds are about $\frac{1}{25}$ inch (1 mm) long, bright orange, oblong, and in one row on each side of the pod.

This is a very common weed on the plains and prairies. Control is similar to other weeds in the rose garden; identify them early, weed them out, and never allow them to go to seed. Closely watch newly planted garden seed, and newly purchased nursery and bedding plants.

Green Foxtail (also known as wild millet, green bristle grass, bottle grass)
Setaria viridis

The stems of green foxtail may be simple or branched, and anywhere up to 3 feet (nearly 1 m) tall depending on the density of the infestation. Leaves are short

Annual poa

Corn spurry

Alberta Agriculture, Food, and Rural Development

Green foxtail

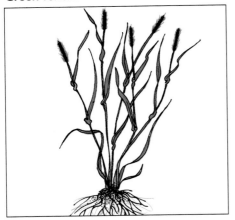

Pineappleweed

Purslane

Alberta Agriculture, Food, and Rural Development

Alberta Agriculture, Food, and Rural Development

and broader than most grasses and look a little like corn as seedlings. Flower spikes may be 1 to 4 inches (2.5 to 10 cm) long, and resemble a rifle cleaner. Green foxtail produces a prolific number of small seeds about $1/16$ inch (1.5 mm) long. It can become a troublesome weed in the garden. A common source of infestation is packaged garden seeds, especially carrots. Plants are easy to pull or hoe making this type of control the recommended practice.

Lamb's-Quarters (also known as pigweed, fat-hen, white goosefoot)
Chenopodium album

This plant will grow anywhere from 1 to 6 feet (30 cm – nearly 2 m). The stems are branched, ridged, and sometimes have reddish lines. Leaves have wavy margins, and the lower surface is a soft gray-green and coated with powdery, mealy particles. Flowers are small, greenish colored, and

Lamb's-quarters

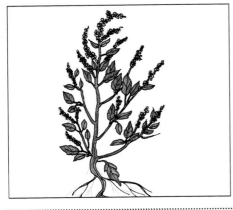

without petals. They are arranged in dense panicles in leaf axils and at the top of the plant. Seeds are $1/20$ inch (under 1 mm) across, shiny, black, flat, and almost round. It is a very common weed that is often introduced through packaged garden seeds or barnyard manure. As with many weeds, the seeds may remain viable in the soil for many years.

Pineappleweed
Matricaria matricarioides

This annual looks very much like many of the mayweeds, but has a pleasant pineapple fragrance when crushed. It grows to 16 inches (40 cm). The leaves are divided several times. Pineappleweed flowers are about ¼ inch (6 mm) across with yellow center florets but no ray flowers (visible petals). It is a prolific seed producer that can become a persistent weed in gardens.

Purslane (also known as pursley, pussley, pusley, wild portulaca)
Portulaca oleracea

This prostrate, fleshy-leafed weed, is troublesome in gardens. The stems are reddish and may be up to 1 foot (30 cm) long. Flowers are small and yellow and appear in clusters at the end of stems and in leaf axils. It is a prolific seed producer, and the seeds may remain viable in the soil for several years. This makes it difficult to control. Packages of mixed flower seeds are common sources of infestation. Purslane

will readily re-establish itself if left on the soil surface after cultivating or hoeing. Plants must be completely removed and destroyed if control is to be successful.

Redroot Pigweed (also known as redroot, rough pigweed, green amaranth)
Amaranthus retroflexus

This annual weed is easily identified by its red or pink taproot. Stems are erect, rough, slightly hairy at the tip, and grow up to 3 feet (nearly 1 m) tall. Leaves are long-stalked, alternate, ovate, slightly hairy, dull green in color, and 2 to 4 inches (5 to 10 cm) long. Flowers are green in dense spikes in leaf axils and on the terminal spike at the top of the plant. Seeds are $1/25$ inch (1 mm) in diameter, almost round, and a glossy jet black. They can lay dormant in the soil for many years, and will germinate when conditions are favorable.

Redroot pigweed

Common chickweed

Alberta Agriculture, Food, and Rural Development

Biennials (Winter Annuals)

Common Chickweed
Stellaria media

Normally, this weed behaves as an annual. Occasionally, plants will survive the winter in areas protected by other plant cover. It is one of the most troublesome weeds in the garden. Usually chickweed grows prostrate or trailing with a line of fine hairs on one side of the stem. The leaves are ¼ to 1 inch (6 mm to 2.5 cm) long. Flowers are white, ¼ inch (6 mm) long, and star-shaped, with five petals. Seeds are in a small capsule, are very small like fine pepper, and very numerous.

Narrow-leaved Hawk's-beard
Crepis tectorum

This hollow-stemmed branching plant on first sight appears like a small slender Perennial Sow Thistle, including the milky juice when broken or bruised. The flowers are small and yellow and up to ¾ inch (2 cm) across. Seeds are ⅛ inch (3 mm) long and attached to a bit of umbrella-like fluff that is easily disseminated throughout the garden. Juvenile plants are difficult to pull and often break off leaving the roots in position to regrow.

Shepherd's Purse
Capsella bursa-pastoris

This weed is only spread by seeds. The stems may be single or branched and up to 20 inches (50 cm) high or more. Leaves are slightly hairy; the basal leaves form a rosette and are deeply cut and lobed. Flowers are small, white, and about ¹/₁₀ inch (2 mm) wide, in terminal racemes. Seed pods are triangular and notched at top, and are ¼ inch (6 mm) long on spreading stalks up to 1 inch (2.5 cm) long. Seeds are ¹/₂₀ inch (less than 1 mm) long. It is a very persistent weed in gardens.

Stinkweed (also known as field pennycress, Frenchweed, fanweed)
Thlaspi arvense

This plant is easily recognized by its unpleasant odor when crushed. The stems are smooth and hairless, from 2 to 18 inches (5 to 45 cm) high, and may be single or branched. The leaves are smooth, hairless, and irregularly toothed. Flowers are small, white, and ⅛ inch (3 mm) across, and form in clusters at the ends of stems. Seed pods are on slim

Narrow-leaved hawk's-beard

Alberta Agriculture, Food, and Rural Development

Shepherd's purse

upward curving stalks. They are oval, flat, and ½ inch (12 mm) across, and turn yellow when ripe. Seeds are ¹/₁₀ inch (2 mm) in diameter, ½ inch (12 mm) long, and a reddish brown to black. Seeds have been known to remain viable in the soil for thirty years.

Stinkweed

Canada Thistle (also known as creeping thistle, field thistle)
Cirsium arvense

This plant is very persistent, with a deep, penetrating root system. Once established, a seedling will grow to take over a square yard (nearly a square metre) in three years or less if no control is used. Stems grow up to over 4 feet (1.5 m), erect, with many branches; leaves are 2 to 6 inches (5 to 15 cm) long, deeply cut, and very prickly. Flowers are up to 1 inch (2.5 cm) in diameter, and vary from purple with a rose tinge to pink. Seeds are ⅛ inch (3 mm) long, dark green and attached to some fluff that is readily blown in the wind.

Common Plantain (also known as broad-leaved plantain, dooryard plantain, birdseed plantain
Plantago major

This perennial plant has tough, tenacious roots that are not easy to pull out. The oval, strongly ribbed leaves are broad and spread out from the crown. Many grow up to 10 inches (25 cm) long. Flowers form a dense narrow spike on a leafless stem, about 4 to 12 inches (10 to 30 cm) long, and resemble a rifle brush. The spike produces numerous ¹/₂₅ inch (1 mm) long, brown or black, egg-shaped seed.

Dandelion
Taraxacum officinale

One of the most common, persistent, and troublesome of garden weeds is the common dandelion. It produces an abundance of seeds, which are up to ¼ inch (6 mm) long, attached to a fluffy, parasol-like appendage, and easily carried and spread by the wind. There isn't a gardener who doesn't know the dandelion, and that the deep fleshy root can sprout from root sections when cut up. This makes it difficult to eradicate by hoeing or other cultivation.

Canada thistle

Perennial Sow Thistle (also known as field sow thistle, creeping sow thistle)
Sonchus arvensis

This is a light green perennial with deep rootstocks that spread out readily like Canada Thistle. The hollow stems may grow up to 5 feet (1.5 m) in height. Leaf margins have soft prickles

Common plantain

Dandelion

and may grow up to 1 foot (30 cm) in length. Stems and leaves exude a milky juice when broken. Bright yellow flowers are up to 1½ inches (nearly 4 cm) in diameter and are grouped loosely on the ends of numerous stalks. The seeds are similar to that of Canada Thistle.

Perennial sow thistle

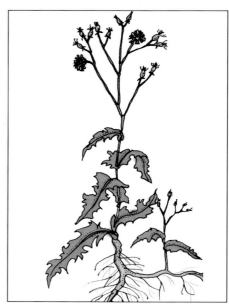

Active ingredients registered for weed control on roses

Weed	chloramben*	dichlobenil	eptc
annual blue grass		✓	✓
annual grass		✓	
barnyard grass	✓		✓
bindweed		✓	
blue aster		✓	
bracken		✓	
broad-leaved weed		✓	
Canada thistle		✓	
carpetweed	✓		
chickweed	✓	✓	
common chickweed			✓
common purslane			✓
crab grass	✓	✓	✓
dandelion		✓	
deadnettle			✓
fall panicum	✓		
foxtail	✓	✓	
giant foxtail			✓
goose grass			✓
grass		✓	
green foxtail			✓
groundsel		✓	
hairy nightshade			✓
horsetail		✓	
johnson grass			✓
knotweed		✓	
kochia		✓	

Weed	chloramben*	dichlobenil	eptc
lamb's-quarters	✓	✓	✓
loosestrife		✓	
love grass			✓
mustard		✓	
nettle-leaved goosefoot			✓
nut sedge		✓	
pigweed	✓	✓	
plantain		✓	
prostrate pigweed			✓
purple nutsedge			✓
purslane	✓	✓	
quack grass		✓	✓
ragweed	✓		
redroot pigweed			✓
sandbur			✓
sheep sorrel		✓	
shepherd's-purse		✓	
smartweed	✓	✓	
sow thistle		✓	
spurge		✓	
tumble pigweed			✓
velvetleaf	✓		
vetch		✓	
wild buckwheat		✓	
wormwood (comprend artemise)		✓	
yellow foxtail			✓
yellow nut sedge			✓

*present as ammonium or sodium salt

Quack grass

Quack Grass (Also known as twitch, quitch, scutch, quick or couch grass)
Agropyron repens

This is one of the worst of the grassy weeds. Quack grass spreads by seed and by underground, creeping stems called rhizomes. Rhizomes are whitish and tough with many nodes that produce new roots and stems. Stems are up to 4 feet (over 1 m) or more tall. Leaves are rough on the surface and have a serrated margin. Flower spikes are green and up to 6 inches (15 cm) in length, and seed spikelets are ½ inch (over 12 mm) in length.

Animal Pest Control

The most common animal pests damaging roses are deer, rabbits, pocket gophers, and mice. Deer, rabbits, and pocket gophers are not common urban pests, but they can be very troublesome in rural areas. Most of the registered domestic chemical animal control products are repellents. Use of toxic compounds may be hazardous to beneficial wildlife, and is severely restricted in most jurisdictions.

Deer and Rabbits

You can take the following steps to control deer and rabbits:

- Build an adequate fence or screen (at least 6 foot (nearly 2 m)) that will keep the deer out of the garden. This fence is more than sufficient for rabbits, if anchored to the ground.
- Keep a dog around the home to discourage these animals from coming near the garden.
- Spray the plants with a repellent such as thiram or any similar product. This product is generally used in fall to protect plants during winter and early spring.
- Use a 30 percent solution of Tabasco and water sprayed on the roses spring and fall to eliminate deer and rabbit damage.

Pocket Gophers (*Thomomys* spp.)

Pocket gophers can do considerable damage to lawns, root vegetables, ornamental bulbs, vines, herbaceous plants, trees, and shrubs including roses. They have also been known to gnaw underground television, telephone, and electrical cables. Flower and vegetable gardens adjacent to wild or agricultural land are most likely to be affected.

The tell-tale mounds are usually the first signs of pocket gopher presence, followed by minor to serious plant damage. They most commonly attack the succulent portions of plant root systems including roses. If not checked, eventually there will be surface damage across the garden, often with entire herbaceous plants being pulled down into the burrows. In an open fall when green vegetation is scarce, pocket gophers have been known to gnaw and girdle green woody plant material at ground level.

In commercial agriculture or horticulture operations, poison bait is often used. In special circumstances, poison gas or pellets are also used. However, for the home gardener, with children and pets in the garden and immediate neighborhood, these are not prudent control measures. Trapping is the accepted method. Special pocket gopher traps are available at local garden centers in areas affected by this pest. Packaging materials usually contain directions on locating the burrows and installing the traps.

Another easy method is using exhaust fumes from a lawn mower, tractor or car. Find the pocket gopher tunnel near the mound. Insert a hose into the tunnel, cover with soil, then connect the other end to the engine exhaust pipe. Run the motor for 5 to 10 minutes. This may have to be repeated as some gophers quickly block off the tunnel.

Mice

Mice can be a problem in both urban and rural areas. They do the greatest damage to roses during the winter, particularly when there is a deep snow cover over long grasses, weeds, or straw mulches. Mice tunnel under the snow along the ground and chew the bark off roses and other sweet tasting shrubs and trees. You may also see mouse damage at the snow surface level. To control mice in and around the garden, build V-troughs made from two pieces of lumber 3 feet (about 1 m) long. One piece should be a 1 × 4 and the other a 1 × 6. The wider board is nailed onto the edge of the narrow board. Invert the V-troughs and place a small tin lid filled with mouse bait beneath the boards. Make several of these and place them strategically in your garden among the shrubs just before snowfall. Mice like to crawl and hide in the protected areas that these bait stations provide. Exercise considerable caution where children or pets may have access to the bait stations.

Deer mice can harbor the dangerous hantavirus disease. Exercise caution when handling the V-troughs or bait containers, and in the disposal of dead mice. Avoid inhaling dust contaminated by mouse droppings and urine. Use a weak chlorine bleach solution to disinfect these items and areas.

Mouse bait station

boards

bait in jar lid

Roses: A Gardener's Guide for the Plains and Prairies

Overwintering Roses

Wintering Tender Roses

Winter protection is absolutely necessary for tender roses on the northern plains and prairies. Resistance to winter kill is dependent upon the variety, with the hardiest being the wild and many varieties of Shrub roses. Among the tender cultivars, the Floribundas generally survive somewhat better than the other so-called tender ones when unprotected.

The following method has proven successful for wintering Hybrid Teas, Grandifloras, Polyanthas, Floribundas, and the tender Shrub roses. These roses do not really fully prepare for winter as our native plants do. They grow and bloom continually until severe cold brings them to a halt. This makes them vulnerable to winter kill. Stop the use of fertilizer after mid-August, and restrict water after mid-September to help them harden off for the winter.

There is one exception to the use of fertilizers after mid to end of August. This is mentioned in the section Fertilizing Roses. At the mid to end of August, use a special winterizing formulation, not for growth but for helping the rose bush to harden off and prepare for winter. It may be worth your while to go back and read that section.

If the soil is dry in late fall (near the end of October), give the rose bushes a good soaking just before winter sets in and the soil freezes. In fact, give all perennials a good soaking at this time. Most years the soil freezes around the end of October or early November. Cut down the rose tops (except the tender Shrub roses) to a height of around 1 foot (30 cm). Destroy the cuttings to prevent the carry-over of diseases and insects that may be present.

The bud graft union requires the most protection. Cover the graft union and the lower canes with insulating material to a minimum depth of about 1 foot (30 cm). The aim of mounding or covering is not to protect them from freezing but to protect them from premature thawing, and repeated freezing and thawing. They may be hilled like potatoes, if they are spaced far enough apart and the rose roots are not exposed by doing this. If they are planted close together, you will have to get soil from some other place, such as a vegetable garden nearby. You can also use peat moss or sawdust which do not freeze and thaw as readily as soil. A large bale of peat moss will cover 8 to 10 rose bushes. If wind is a problem, cover the hills with a bit of hay, straw, spruce boughs, or better still, burlap/gunny sack material. In places where neatness, tidiness, and fire hazards are of no major concern, use

Roses covered with peat moss

Roses covered with peat moss and burlap

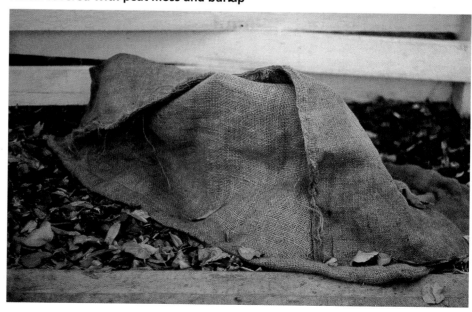

Straw covering

straw or hay over the peat moss to a depth of about 1 foot (30 cm). Dust powdered sulfur over each plant to discourage mice, remembering that the sulfur can change soil pH.

An alternative for those who have only a few tender rose bushes is the use of large fiber pots, at least 1 foot (30 cm) in diameter, commonly used for potting trees and large shrubs by nurseries. Cut the bottom out, invert it, position it over the rose bush, and fill it with peat moss, saw dust, or other material.

A good snow cover adds considerable protection. On roses where the snow cover is thin, you can spread sidewalk, driveway, or drifted snow over them. Do not use snow that has had a chemical de-icer applied to it.

During mild spells you may have difficulty keeping an adequate snow cover on rose beds in front of south facing buildings or other structures. It is not the cold that kills rose bushes but the repeated freezing and thawing that occurs in early spring. The covering recommended above should keep the soil frozen until the final spring thaw.

Planting with the graft union 4 inches (10 cm) below ground level permits the use of minimum coverage and at the same time provides sufficient winter protection. Using the recommended method, the author rarely loses more than a few roses out of over 300 grown each year. Most of those lost are eight years old or older. Since it is not definitively known how long tender roses are likely to live on the northern plains and prairies, these may have died of old age. The author has quite a number of rose bushes 25 to 30 years old that were planted and protected as recommended.

Overcoming Planting Problems

The advice and instructions for planting on packaged roses are usually meant for rose growers in areas where winters are very mild.

If roses have been planted with the graft union above the ground level as recommended in most books, or as shown on containers of packaged roses, one of the following methods will have to be used to get them through the winter safely.

Method 1:

After the frost has killed the foliage, cut the canes down to about 1 foot (30 cm) in height. Label the plants by attaching a water-proof marker to the bushes. Dig them up and bury them in the garden or some other convenient spot at a depth of 1 to 2 feet (30 to 60 cm). Be certain that you do not bury them where water is likely to pool after a spring thaw. In spring when the tree buds are about to burst into leaf, dig them up and replant. Digging the roses in this manner destroys a lot of the fine roots and sets them back significantly.

Method 2:

After the frost has killed the foliage, cover the plants with insulating material such as hay, peat moss, sawdust, or wheat straw to a depth of 2 feet (60 cm). In spring when the native trees are about to burst into leaf, uncover, prune, and clean up.

Removal of Winter Protective Cover

This is an important spring chore often overlooked, especially where soil is used as a covering for winter protection. Remove covering some time between early April and the end of April depending on how early the native tree buds are starting to burst out into leaf. You will probably be able to recover about 80 percent of your original covering provided you have not lost any due to wind erosion.

Around each rose bush, hollow out a shallow depression 1 to 1½ feet (30 to 45 cm) in diameter and about 2 inches (5 cm) deep to facilitate the emergence of new shoots from below ground, plus watering and fertilizing.

Many good roses are weakened and actually lost because of the failure to remove soil covering the bush.

Occasionally there may be a threatening frost after the roses are uncovered. Should this happen, be prepared to cover your bushes with burlap, paper, large fiber pots, or canvas tarp. Burlap is perhaps best because it is a good insulator and is easy to handle, store, and re-use.

Burlap removed in spring

Peat moss removed

Wintering Potted Roses

Potted roses may be wintered successfully by using one of two methods.

Method 1:

Perhaps the safest and easiest method is to dig a trench up to 2 feet (60 cm) deep, and lay the plant and pot down horizontally in the trench. Then completely cover with moist soil, peat moss, or sawdust. The main idea is to have at least 1 foot (30 cm) or more of cover over the roots and canes. Tie canes firmly together with a twine. This makes it a lot easier to lay them down and dig them out in the spring. In early spring, dig them up and begin standard maintenance procedures.

Method 2:

If you are fortunate enough to have access to a root house, you have a good place to overwinter potted roses. Just prior to complete freeze-up, store the rose, pot and all, in the root house. Check periodically during the winter to make certain they do not dry out. In the spring, replace up to 3 inches (7.5 cm) of the surface soil, water the plant, and it is off to another good start.

Wintering Standard Tree Roses

Standard or Tree roses are considerably more difficult to winter than Hybrid Teas or Floribundas. Their graft union is on a single stem (standard) at between 3 and 4 feet (about 1 m) above the root system. To successfully overwinter Standard roses, the graft union must be protected with at least 1 foot (30 cm) of soil or some other insulating material.

To provide this protection, you must follow one of two methods.

Method 1:

Plant in a normal way. In the fall, when frost threatens to kill all growth, dig them out with as much of the root system as possible. Bury them horizontally with moist soil or peat moss in a pit up to 2 feet (60) deep. In early spring dig them up and replant. See above for Wintering Potted Roses.

Method 2:

Plant the roses in as large a container as you can handle. In the fall, at about freeze-up time, either bury them horizontally or store in a root house as suggested previously for other potted roses.

Tools for the Rose Gardener

Gardening tools should be viewed as a long-lasting investment. The best advice is to buy good tools. When not in use, keep them clean and under cover so that the wooden handles do not deteriorate and the metal does not rust. At the end of the season, rub all metal parts with an oiled cloth and wooden handles with linseed oil.

Spade

A spade for the garden is like a plow for the farm. It is a heavy duty tool used in the preparation of rose beds and for digging planting holes. A narrow-nosed spade is used for digging in confined areas. Sharpen a spade regularly for easier digging. There are gardeners who say "shovel" for "spade" and vice versa. Those who want to be correct will use a "spade" to dig with (it has a sharp, pointed blade). A "shovel" has a straight, flat blade and is designed to shovel gravel, grain, snow and loose soil; it is not designed for digging.

Spades and trowels

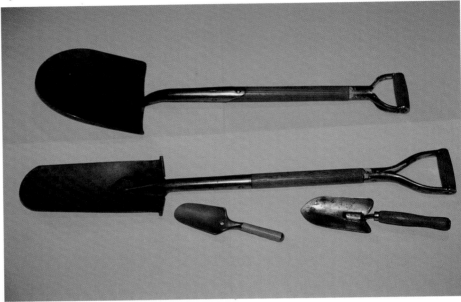

Rake

A rake is mainly used for cleaning up loose debris, breaking up soil lumps, and levelling rose beds in preparation for planting.

Hand Trowel

This is a useful tool for soil mixing, filling in the holes when planting roses, and dishing out the basin-like depressions at the base of rose bushes to facilitate watering and fertilizing.

Hoe

The purpose of the common garden hoe is for cultivating and keeping weeds down. You may have used a standard hoe and found that, within a day or two, many weeds were recovering from the hoeing. Actually they may have been covered with soil or transplanted. If you have had this problem, you'll appreciate the Super Weeder illustrated here. Not only will it cut weeds by pushing and pulling, but it also leaves the weeds loose on the surface. For years this type of hoe was not available commercially, but it has now appeared in the market place. Plans for making this type and a smaller model are given in the Resource Materials section.

Super weeder

Pruning tools

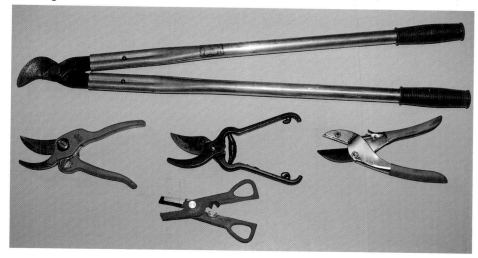

Wheelbarrow

When you start working in the garden, you'll need to move discarded soil and sub-soil and bring in your soil mix. You can prepare a soil mix in the wheelbarrow if you wish. If you do not like the one-wheeler, which tips easily, there is a very handy, very manouverable two-wheel cart available.

Gloves

Gloves are absolutely necessary when working with roses. Those with leather palms and heavy duty, thorn-proof, cotton backs work well. Good leather gloves are better but much more expensive.

Pruners

There are many types of pruners on the market. The best for the rose gardener are the scissor-action type. When sharp, they make a clean cut. The anvil type have the tendency to crush the rose cane, especially if they are not sharp. The long-handled pruners (loppers) are used for heavy canes and difficult work where it is not convenient to use a saw.

Duster

Dusters come in a great variety of types and sizes. As with sprayers, get one to match your garden: a small one for a few plants and a larger one for a bigger garden. The one shown here is suitable for small and average home gardens. Another thing that is unique about this duster is that it can also be used as a small sprayer. It does not corrode, rust, or clog. It is easy to load or empty just by removing the end cap.

Sprayer

Sprayers are available in many types and sizes, ranging from the hand-sized, trigger-operated unit up to hand pump, back pack, and even larger ones mounted on a cart, pressurized by motor, battery, or electric power. The hand-sized sprayer may be adequate for anyone with no more than half a dozen rose bushes. The 1 U.S. gallon (3 to 4 L) size may be good for up to 20 to 25 bushes and the 3 U.S. gallon (10 L) size for 50 or more rose bushes. When buying a sprayer, choose one made of plastic or stainless steel. Clean it out after every use and it will be trouble-free and last a long time. The sprayer in the photograph is stainless steel. It has been used for thirty years and looks good enough to last another ten years.

Water Hose

Anyone with more than six rose bushes needs a water hose. The length required depends on how far the roses are from the water source. Whatever the length, get a cord-reinforced rubber hose. You will pay a little more for this than for a plastic one, but you'll have no problems with stiff, hard-to-handle plastic. You will also find that it will outlast several plastic hoses.

Water Wand

The wand can be fitted with water breakers for fine, medium, and coarse, gentle rain-like watering. It can also be fitted with a nozzle that forces a strong upward spray, which is useful for the control of spider mites. The wands come in various lengths.

Water Pails and Barrels

Metal or plastic pails of a size convenient for you are very handy for carrying water and preparing fertilizer solutions. Containers or barrels as large as feasible for preparing alfalfa and cow tea are required by anyone growing 100 rose bushes or more.

Sprayer and duster

Name Stakes

There are many kinds of name stakes you can buy at garden shops. You can also make your own stakes. Cut them out of 1 inch (2.5 cm) thick cedar lumber, 1 foot (30 cm) long, and ¼ inch (6 mm) thick on a fine-toothed power circular bench saw. The stakes come out very smooth and require no sanding. Sharpen them at one end, dip them in a green wood preservative, and allow them to dry before use. Print the name of the rose on them using a water-proof marker, china marker, or a thick soft-lead beginner's pencil, and you have a good, long-lasting name stake. Cedar stakes last for several years and are inconspicuous in the garden. When the lettering becomes faded, it can be renewed by a light sanding and re-writing.

Plant Support Stakes

Bamboo stakes, up to 4 feet (1.2 m) in height, are long-lasting and the best for supporting rose bush canes. However, much more inexpensive stakes can be made from willow saplings found along roadside ditches in wooded areas. When dried, and dipped in a wood preservative, they will last three years or longer.

Twist-Ties

Plastic coated twist-ties in dispensing rolls are handy for every gardener, especially rose growers. They may be cut to any required length. They are ideal for securing weak, long, and heavily-laden canes to stakes. The plastic-coated kind, if saved, can be used for many years.

Rose Bed Cover

A cover made of porous material is required for the rose bed during the winterization process. After the peat moss has been applied in late fall, the bushes are then covered to prevent the

Name stakes and twist-ties

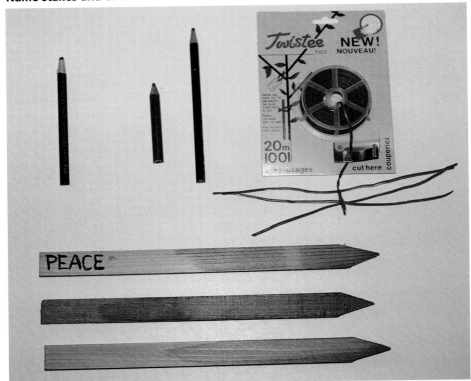

peat moss from being blown away by the wind. For a few rose bushes, an old bed sheet will work. For larger numbers, burlap sacking material is the best. It will last up to five years provided that after use it is dried and stored in a dry place.

Knee Pads

Knee pads provide comfort for gardeners when planting roses or when kneeling and doing other gardening tasks.

Peat Storage Box

Obtain a box large enough to hold the peat moss or other covering used to protect your rose bushes over winter. You may be surprised at how much covering material can be recovered. For 100 roses, the dimension of the box would have to be at least 35 to 40 cubic feet (1 cubic metre). Base the size of the storage box on the number of roses you

grow. If you don't have a box, peat moss may be held over from one year to the next, in the original plastic bags if they have not been badly damaged. Once you have winterized your roses, you will have a good idea of what size storage box or boxes are needed. If the peat moss cannot be saved in the spring, you will have to buy more peat moss every year.

Rain Gauge

In order to determine the amount of supplementary water required each week, use a rain gauge or other straight sided container. Place the gauge in an open unsheltered area.

Radio, TV, and Internet reports provide only regional or district rainfall averages, and there is often a sizeable difference between these figures and the actual rainfall at any given location. Keep your own records and water the roses accordingly.

Chapter Four
Selected Roses

Growing roses in this part of the world can be a challenging job. By following the guidelines set out in the previous chapters and selecting hardy roses, you will be well on your way to the beautiful garden you have imagined.

Selected Roses

The following pages contain a listing of rose cultivars that have proven to be hardy in the author's experience. They are organized alphabetically by their common name within their rose category.

An explanation of the icons and how to find the information you are looking for is found on the next page.

What the icons mean

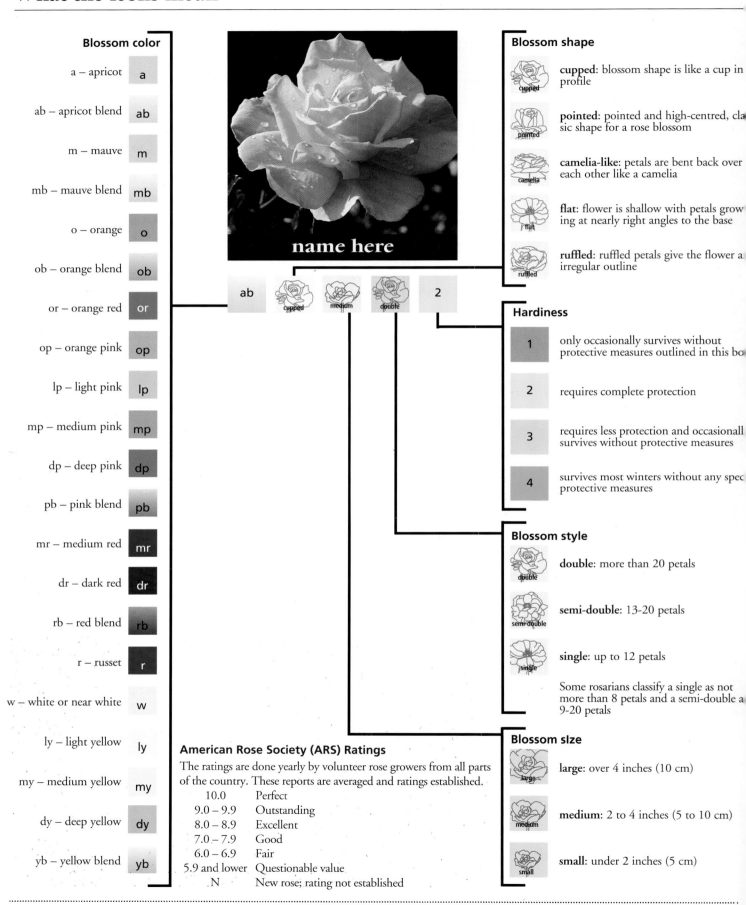

Blossom color

a – apricot	a
ab – apricot blend	ab
m – mauve	m
mb – mauve blend	mb
o – orange	o
ob – orange blend	ob
or – orange red	or
op – orange pink	op
lp – light pink	lp
mp – medium pink	mp
dp – deep pink	dp
pb – pink blend	pb
mr – medium red	mr
dr – dark red	dr
rb – red blend	rb
r – russet	r
w – white or near white	w
ly – light yellow	ly
my – medium yellow	my
dy – deep yellow	dy
yb – yellow blend	yb

name here

ab   cupped   medium   double   2

Blossom shape

cupped: blossom shape is like a cup in profile

pointed: pointed and high-centred, classic shape for a rose blossom

camelia-like: petals are bent back over each other like a camelia

flat: flower is shallow with petals growing at nearly right angles to the base

ruffled: ruffled petals give the flower a irregular outline

Hardiness

1	only occasionally survives without protective measures outlined in this bo
2	requires complete protection
3	requires less protection and occasionall survives without protective measures
4	survives most winters without any spec protective measures

Blossom style

double: more than 20 petals

semi-double: 13-20 petals

single: up to 12 petals

Some rosarians classify a single as not more than 8 petals and a semi-double a 9-20 petals

Blossom size

large: over 4 inches (10 cm)

medium: 2 to 4 inches (5 to 10 cm)

small: under 2 inches (5 cm)

American Rose Society (ARS) Ratings

The ratings are done yearly by volunteer rose growers from all parts of the country. These reports are averaged and ratings established.

10.0	Perfect
9.0 – 9.9	Outstanding
8.0 – 8.9	Excellent
7.0 – 7.9	Good
6.0 – 6.9	Fair
5.9 and lower	Questionable value
N	New rose; rating not established

Blaze

mr	cupped	medium	semi-double	2

Continuity of bloom: free and abundant
Fragrance: slight fragrance
Growing height: tall
ARS rating: 7.2
Performance at shows: A

Dartmund

mr	flat	large	single	4

Continuity of bloom: free and abundant
Fragrance: very fragrant
Growing height: tall
ARS rating: 9.4
Performance at shows: B

Goldstar

dy	flat	large	double	2

Continuity of bloom: free and abundant
Fragrance: slight fragrance
Growing height: tall
ARS rating: 7.0
Performance at shows: A

Henry Kelsey K

mr	cupped	medium	double	4

Continuity of bloom: free and abundant
Fragrance: very fragrant
Growing height: tall
ARS rating: N
Performance at shows: rarely shown

John Cabot K

mr	cupped	medium	double	4

Continuity of bloom: free and abundant
Fragrance: very fragrant
Growing height: tall
ARS rating: 9.4
Performance at shows: A

Morning Jewel

mp	cupped	large	semi-double	2

Continuity of bloom: free and abundant
Fragrance: slight fragrance
Growing height: tall
ARS rating: 7.5
Performance at shows: A

Climbers

Rosarium Uetersen

| dp | camelia | medium | double | 2 |

Continuity of bloom: free and abundant
Fragrance: slight fragrance
Growing height: tall
ARS rating: 8.5
Performance at shows: A

Floribunda

Anne Cocker

| op | pointed | medium | double | 2 |

Continuity of bloom: moderate
Fragrance: no fragrance
Growing height: medium
ARS rating: 7.2
Performance at shows: A

Apache Tears

| rb | pointed | medium | double | 2 |

Continuity of bloom: free and abundant
Fragrance: slight fragrance
Growing height: medium
ARS rating: 7.0
Performance at shows: B

Arthur Bell

| my | pointed | large | semi-double | 2 |

Continuity of bloom: free and abundant
Fragrance: very fragrant
Growing height: tall
ARS rating: 7.5
Performance at shows: A

Atco Royale

| my | pointed | medium | double | 2 |

Continuity of bloom: free and abundant
Fragrance: slight fragrance
Growing height: medium
ARS rating: N
Performance at shows: B

Betty Prior

| mp | cupped | medium | single | 2 |

Continuity of bloom: free and abundant
Fragrance: slight fragrance
Growing height: medium
ARS rating: 8.2
Performance at shows: A

Bon Bon

| pb | cupped | large | semi-double | 2 |

Continuity of bloom: moderate
Fragrance: slight fragrance
Growing height: short
ARS rating: 7.5
Performance at shows: B

Burma Star

| ab | cupped | large | double | 2 |

Continuity of bloom: free and abundant
Fragrance: slight fragrance
Growing height: tall
ARS rating: 8.5
Performance at shows: A

Cathedral

| ab | pointed | large | double | 2 |

Continuity of bloom: moderate
Fragrance: slight fragrance
Growing height: medium
ARS rating: 7.5
Performance at shows: A

Cathedral Splendor

| mp | cupped | large | double | 2 |

Continuity of bloom: free and abundant
Fragrance: slight fragrance
Growing height: medium
ARS rating: N
Performance at shows: B

Crathes Castle

| mp | cupped | large | semi-double | 2 |

Continuity of bloom: free and abundant
Fragrance: slight fragrance
Growing height: medium
ARS rating: 8.5
Performance at shows: A

Dearest

| pb | pointed | large | double | 2 |

Continuity of bloom: free and abundant
Fragrance: medium fragrance
Growing height: medium
ARS rating: 7.2
Performance at shows: A

Dicky

| op | pointed | large | double | 2 |

Continuity of bloom: free and abundant
Fragrance: slight fragrance
Growing height: medium
ARS rating: 8.8
Performance at shows: A

Elizabeth of Glamis

| op | pointed | large | double | 2 |

Continuity of bloom: free and abundant
Fragrance: very fragrant
Growing height: tall
ARS rating: 7.5
Performance at shows: A

Escapade

| m | cupped | medium | single | 2 |

Continuity of bloom: free and abundant
Fragrance: slight fragrance
Growing height: medium
ARS rating: 8.7
Performance at shows: A

Europeana

| dr | flat | medium | double | 2 |

Continuity of bloom: free and abundant
Fragrance: slight fragrance
Growing height: medium
ARS rating: 9.0
Performance at shows: A

Evelyn Fison

| mr | cupped | medium | double | 2 |

Continuity of bloom: free and abundant
Fragrance: slight fragrance
Growing height: medium
ARS rating: 7.8
Performance at shows: B

Eyepaint

| rb | flat | medium | single | 2 |

Continuity of bloom: free and abundant
Fragrance: slightly fragrant
Growing height: medium
ARS rating: 8.5
Performance at shows: A

French Lace

| w | cupped | medium | double | 2 |

Continuity of bloom: moderate
Fragrance: slight fragrance
Growing height: medium
ARS rating: 8.3
Performance at shows: A

Fresco

| ob | pointed | medium | double | 2 |

Continuity of bloom: free and abundant
Fragrance: slight fragrance
Growing height: medium
ARS rating: 8.5
Performance at shows: A

Ginger

| or | cupped | medium | double | 2 |

Continuity of bloom: free and abundant
Fragrance: slight fragrance
Growing height: medium
ARS rating: 7.4
Performance at shows: B

Golden Slippers

| yb | cupped | medium | double | 2 |

Continuity of bloom: free and abundant
Fragrance: slight fragrance
Growing height: medium
ARS rating: 7.6
Performance at shows: A

Iceberg

| w | cupped | medium | double | 2 |

Continuity of bloom: free and abundant
Fragrance: very fragrant
Growing height: medium
ARS rating: 8.9
Performance at shows: A

Impatient

| or | camelia | medium | double | 2 |

Continuity of bloom: free and abundant
Fragrance: slightly fragrant
Growing height: medium
ARS rating: 7.7
Performance at shows: A

Interama

dr	cupped	large	semi-double	2

Continuity of bloom: free and abundant
Fragrance: slight fragrance
Growing height: medium
ARS rating: 7.6
Performance at shows: B

International Herald Tribune

m	cupped	medium	double	2

Continuity of bloom: free and abundant
Fragrance: very fragrant
Growing height: short
ARS rating: 8.0
Performance at shows: A

Intrigue

m	pointed	large	double	2

Continuity of bloom: moderate
Fragrance: very fragrant
Growing height: medium
ARS rating: 7.5
Performance at shows: A

Little Darling

yb	cupped	medium	double	2

Continuity of bloom: free and abundant
Fragrance: moderate fragrance
Growing height: medium
ARS rating: 8.3
Performance at shows: A

Lively Lady

or	cupped	medium	double	2

Continuity of bloom: free and abundant
Fragrance: slight fragrance
Growing height: medium
ARS rating: 8.0
Performance at shows: rarely shown

Liverpool Echo

op	pointed	medium	double	2

Continuity of bloom: free and abundant
Fragrance: slight fragrance
Growing height: medium
ARS rating: 7.6
Performance at shows: A

Livin' Easy (Fellowship)

| ob | cupped | medium | double | 2 |

Continuity of bloom:	free and abundant
Fragrance:	slight fragrance
Growing height:	medium
ARS rating:	8.0
Performance at shows:	A

Margaret Merril

| w | cupped | medium | double | 2 |

Continuity of bloom:	free and abundant
Fragrance:	medium fragrance
Growing height:	medium
ARS rating:	8.5
Performance at shows:	B

Nana Mouskouri

| w | pointed | large | double | 2 |

Continuity of bloom:	free and abundant
Fragrance:	medum fragrance
Growing height:	medium
ARS rating:	8.2
Performance at shows:	B

Nicole

| w | cupped | medium | double | 2 |

Continuity of bloom:	moderate
Fragrance:	slight fragrance
Growing height:	medium
ARS rating:	9.2
Performance at shows:	B

Priscilla Burton

| rb | flat | medium | semi-double | 2 |

Continuity of bloom:	free and abundant
Fragrance:	medium fragrance
Growing height:	medium
ARS rating:	8.7
Performance at shows:	A

Rob Roy

| dr | pointed | large | double | 2 |

Continuity of bloom:	free and abundant
Fragrance:	slight fragrance
Growing height:	medium
ARS rating:	8.0
Performance at shows:	A

Royal Occasion (Montana)

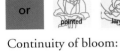

Continuity of bloom:	free and abundant
Fragrance:	slight fragrance
Growing height:	medium
ARS rating:	8.6
Performance at shows:	B

Rumba

Continuity of bloom:	free and abundant
Fragrance:	medium fragrance
Growing height:	medium
ARS rating:	5.6
Performance at shows:	B

Sarabande

Continuity of bloom:	free and abundant
Fragrance:	slight fragrance
Growing height:	medium
ARS rating:	7.8
Performance at shows:	A

Scentimental

Continuity of bloom:	free and abundant
Fragrance:	very fragrant
Growing height:	medium
ARS rating:	N
Performance at shows:	A

Sea Pearl

Continuity of bloom:	free and abundant
Fragrance:	slight fragrance
Growing height:	medium
ARS rating:	7.4
Performance at shows:	A

Sexy Rexy

Continuity of bloom:	free and abundant
Fragrance:	slight fragrance
Growing height:	medium
ARS rating:	9.0
Performance at shows:	A

Simplicity

| mp | flat | large | semi-double | 2 |

Continuity of bloom: free and abundant
Fragrance: slight fragrance
Growing height: medium
ARS rating: 8.0
Performance at shows: A

St. John

| w | cupped | medium | double | 2 |

Continuity of bloom: free and abundant
Fragrance: slight fragrance
Growing height: medium
ARS rating: N
Performance at shows: rarely shown

Sue Lawley

| rb | flat | medium | semi-double | 2 |

Continuity of bloom: free and abundant
Fragrance: slight fragrance
Growing height: medium
ARS rating: 7.5
Performance at shows: A

Sunsprite (Korresia)

| dy | cupped | medium | double | 2 |

Continuity of bloom: free and abundant
Fragrance: very fragrant
Growing height: short
ARS rating: 8.7
Performance at shows: A

The Sun

| or | cupped | large | semi-double | 2 |

Continuity of bloom: free and abundant
Fragrance: slight fragrance
Growing height: medium
ARS rating: 8.5
Performance at shows: B

Traumerei

| ob | flat | large | double | 2 |

Continuity of bloom: free and abundant
Fragrance: very fragrant
Growing height: medium
ARS rating: 7.9
Performance at shows: B

Floribunda

Trumpeter

Viva

or · cupped · large · double · 2

dr · pointed · medium · double · 2

Continuity of bloom:	free and abundant		Continuity of bloom:	free and abundant
Fragrance:	slight fragrance		Fragrance:	slight fragrance
Growing height:	medium		Growing height:	medium
ARS rating:	8.0		ARS rating:	8.0
Performance at shows:	A		Performance at shows:	A

Grandiflora

Alaska Centennial

Caribbean

Comanche

dr · pointed · large · double · 2

ab · pointed · large · double · 2

or · pointed · medium · double · 2

Continuity of bloom:	free and abundant		Continuity of bloom:	free and abundant		Continuity of bloom:	free and abundant
Fragrance:	slight fragrance		Fragrance:	slight fragrance		Fragrance:	slight fragrance
Growing height:	medium		Growing height:	medium		Growing height:	medium
ARS rating:	8.5		ARS rating:	7.2		ARS rating:	7.5
Performance at shows:	B		Performance at shows:	A		Performance at shows:	A

Grandiflora

Flamingo Queen

| dp | pointed | large | double | 2 |

Continuity of bloom: free and abundant
Fragrance: slight fragrance
Growing height: medium
ARS rating: 8.8
Performance at shows: B

Olé

| or | pointed | large | double | 2 |

Continuity of bloom: free and abundant
Fragrance: slight fragrance
Growing height: tall
ARS rating: 7.0
Performance at shows: A

Pink Parfait

| pb | pointed | medium | double | 2 |

Continuity of bloom: free and abundant
Fragrance: slight fragrance
Growing height: medium
ARS rating: 8.1
Performance at shows: A

Prominent

| or | cupped | medium | double | 2 |

Continuity of bloom: moderate
Fragrance: slight fragrance
Growing height: medium
ARS rating: 7.1
Performance at shows: A

Queen Elizabeth

| mp | pointed | large | double | 2 |

Continuity of bloom: free and abundant
Fragrance: slight fragrance
Growing height: tall
ARS rating: 7.4
Performance at shows: A

Scarlet Knight

| mr | pointed | large | double | 2 |

Continuity of bloom: free and abundant
Fragrance: slight fragrance
Growing height: medium
ARS rating: 7.0
Performance at shows: B

Hybrid Tea

Adolf Horstmann

| yb | pointed | large | double | 2 |

Continuity of bloom: free and abundant
Fragrance: slight fragrance
Growing height: medium
ARS rating: 7.5
Performance at shows: B

Amazing Grace

| mp | pointed | large | double | 2 |

Continuity of bloom: moderate
Fragrance: slight fragrance
Growing height: medium
ARS rating: 8.0
Performance at shows: B

Athena

| w | pointed | large | double | 2 |

Continuity of bloom: free and abundant
Fragrance: slight fragrance
Growing height: medium
ARS rating: 7.0
Performance at shows: rarely shown

Audrey Hepburn

| lp | pointed | large | double | 2 |

Continuity of bloom: free and abundant
Fragrance: medium fragrance
Growing height: medium
ARS rating: 7.7
Performance at shows: rarely shown

Ave Maria

| op | pointed | large | double | 2 |

Continuity of bloom: free and abundant
Fragrance: slight fragrance
Growing height: medium
ARS rating: 7.4
Performance at shows: B

Barkarole

| dr | pointed | large | double | 2 |

Continuity of bloom: free and abundant
Fragrance: medium fragrance
Growing height: tall
ARS rating: 7.5
Performance at shows: Rarely shown

Bel Ange

mp	pointed	medium	double	2

Continuity of bloom: free and abundant
Fragrance: very fragrant
Growing height: medium
ARS rating: 7.2
Performance at shows: B

Berolina (Selfridges)

dy	pointed	large	double	2

Continuity of bloom: free and abundant
Fragrance: very fragrant
Growing height: tall
ARS rating: N (Author's 7.7)
Performance at shows: A

Bobby Charlton

pb	pointed	large	double	2

Continuity of bloom: moderate
Fragrance: medium fragrance
Growing height: medium
ARS rating: 7.1
Performance at shows: B

Brigadoon

pb	pointed	large	double	2

Continuity of bloom: free and abundant
Fragrance: medium fragrance
Growing height: medium
ARS rating: 7.3
Performance at shows: A

Burgund '81 (Loving Memory)

dr	pointed	large	double	2

Continuity of bloom: free and abundant
Fragrance: very fragrant
Growing height: medium
ARS rating: 7.1
Performance at shows: B

Captain Harry Stebbings

dp	pointed	large	double	2

Continuity of bloom: free and abundant
Fragrance: very fragrant
Growing height: medium
ARS rating: 8.1
Performance at shows: B

Chicago Peace

| pb | pointed | large | double | 2 |

Continuity of bloom: free and abundant
Fragrance: slight fragrance
Growing height: medium
ARS rating: 7.5
Performance at shows: B

Chrysler Imperial

| dr | pointed | large | double | 2 |

Continuity of bloom: moderate
Fragrance: very fragrant
Growing height: medium
ARS rating: 7.5
Performance at shows: A

Clarita

| or | pointed | large | double | 2 |

Continuity of bloom: free and abundant
Fragrance: slight fragrance
Growing height: medium
ARS rating: 7.5
Performance at shows: B

Color Magic

| pb | pointed | large | double | 2 |

Continuity of bloom: moderate
Fragrance: slight fragrance
Growing height: medium
ARS rating: 8.2
Performance at shows: A

Corso

| ob | pointed | large | double | 2 |

Continuity of bloom: moderate
Fragrance: slight fragrance
Growing height: medium
ARS rating: 7.0
Performance at shows: B

Dainty Bess

| lp | flat | large | single | 2 |

Continuity of bloom: moderate
Fragrance: medium fragrance
Growing height: medium
ARS rating: 8.9
Performance at shows: A

Dolly Parton

| or | 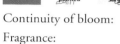 | | | 2 |

Continuity of bloom: moderate
Fragrance: very fragran
Growing height: medium
ARS rating: 7.3
Performance at shows: A

Doris Tysterman

| ob | | | | 2 |

Continuity of bloom: free and abundant
Fragrance: slight fragrance
Growing height: medium
ARS rating: 7.0
Performance at shows: B

Double Delight

| rb | | | | 2 |

Continuity of bloom: free and abundant
Fragrance: very fragrant
Growing height: medium
ARS rating: 8
Performance at shows: A

Dr. Brownell

| yb | | | | 3 |

Continuity of bloom: free and abundant
Fragrance: very fragrant
Growing height: medium
ARS rating: 6.1
Performance at shows: B

Duet

| mp | | | | 2 |

Continuity of bloom: free and abundant
Fragrance: slight fragrance
Growing height: medium
ARS rating: 7.3
Performance at shows: A

Duftzauber

| mr | | | | 2 |

Continuity of bloom: free and abundant
Fragrance: very fragrant
Growing height: medium
ARS rating: 8.0
Performance at shows: A

Dutch Gold

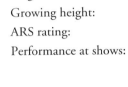

Electron

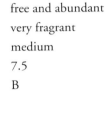

Elina (Peau Douce)

my	pointed	large	double	2

Continuity of bloom: moderate
Fragrance: slight fragrance
Growing height: medium
ARS rating: 5.8
Performance at shows: B

dp	pointed	large	double	2

Continuity of bloom: free and abundant
Fragrance: very fragrant
Growing height: medium
ARS rating: 7.5
Performance at shows: B

ly	pointed	large	double	2

Continuity of bloom: free and abundant
Fragrance: medium fragrance
Growing height: medium
ARS rating: 8.9
Performance at shows: A

Elizabeth Taylor

Folklore

Fragrant Cloud

dp	pointed	large	double	2

Continuity of bloom: moderate
Fragrance: slight fragrance
Growing height: medium
ARS rating: 8.9
Performance at shows: A

ab	pointed	large	double	2

Continuity of bloom: free and abundant
Fragrance: very fragrant
Growing height: tall
ARS rating: 8.5
Performance at shows: A

or	pointed	large	double	2

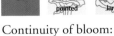

Continuity of bloom: moderate
Fragrance: very fragrant
Growing height: medium
ARS rating: 8.1
Performance at shows: A

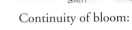

Fragrant Memory (Jadis)

| mp | pointed | large | double | 2 |

Continuity of bloom:	moderate
Fragrance:	very fragrant
Growing height:	medium
ARS rating:	7.1
Performance at shows:	A

Gail Borden

| pb | pointed | large | double | 2 |

Continuity of bloom:	moderate
Fragrance:	medium fragrance
Growing height:	medium
ARS rating:	7.0
Performance at shows:	B

Garden Party

| w | pointed | large | double | 2 |

Continuity of bloom:	free and abundant
Fragrance:	slight fragrance
Growing height:	medium
ARS rating:	8.1
Performance at shows:	A

Golden Jubilee

| my | pointed | large | double | 2 |

Continuity of bloom:	free and abundant
Fragrance:	medium fragrance
Growing height:	medium
ARS rating:	7.5
Performance at shows:	B

Harmonie

| op | pointed | large | double | 2 |

Continuity of bloom:	moderate
Fragrance:	very fragrant
Growing height:	medium
ARS rating:	7.0
Performance at shows:	A

Holsteinperle

| op | pointed | large | double | 2 |

Continuity of bloom:	free and abundant
Fragrance:	no fragrance
Growing height:	tall
ARS rating:	7.5
Performance at shows:	B

Honor

| w |  pointed | large | double | 2 |

Continuity of bloom: free and abundant
Fragrance: medium fragrance
Growing height: medium
ARS rating: 7.6
Performance at shows: B

Ingrid Bergman

| dr | pointed | large | double | 2 |

Continuity of bloom: free and abundant
Fragrance: medium fragrance
Growing height: medium
ARS rating: 7.1
Performance at shows: B

Jane Pauley

| ob | pointed | large | double | 2 |

Continuity of bloom: free and abundant
Fragrance: medium fragrance
Growing height: medium
ARS rating: 7.1
Performance at shows: A

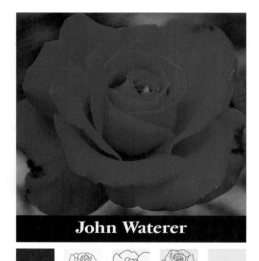

John Waterer

| dr | pointed | large | double | 2 |

Continuity of bloom: free and abundant
Fragrance: slight fragrance
Growing height: medium
ARS rating: 7.9
Performance at shows: B

Just Joey

| ob | pointed | large | double | 2 |

Continuity of bloom: moderate
Fragrance: very fragrant
Growing height: medium
ARS rating: 7.9
Performance at shows: B

Keepsake (Esmeralda)

| pb | pointed | large | double | 2 |

Continuity of bloom: somewhat "stingy"
Fragrance: medium fragrance
Growing height: medium
ARS rating: 8.4
Performance at shows: A

Hybrid Tea

Kings Ransom

Konrad Henkel

Kordes Perfecta

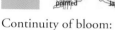

| dy | pointed | large | double | 2 |

Continuity of bloom: moderate
Fragrance: slight fragrance
Growing height: medium
ARS rating: 6.2
Performance at shows: B

| mr | pointed | large | double | 2 |

Continuity of bloom: free and abundant
Fragrance: medium fragrance
Growing height: medium
ARS rating: 8.0
Performance at shows: B

| pb | pointed | large | double | 2 |

Continuity of bloom: moderate
Fragrance: very fragrant
Growing height: medium
ARS rating: 6.5
Performance at shows: A

Lady Diana

Las Vegas

Lolita

| lp | pointed | medium | double | 2 |

Continuity of bloom: moderate
Fragrance: slight fragrance
Growing height: medium
ARS rating: 8.0
Performance at shows: B

| ob | pointed | large | double | 2 |

Continuity of bloom: moderate
Fragrance: slight fragrance
Growing height: medium
ARS rating: 6.0
Performance at shows: B

| ab | pointed | large | double | 2 |

Continuity of bloom: free and abundant
Fragrance: very fragrant
Growing height: medium
ARS rating: 7.5
Performance at shows: B

Lucy Cramphorn

Lustige

Maria Stern

| or | pointed | large | double | 2 |

Continuity of bloom: free and abundant
Fragrance: medium fragrance
Growing height: medium
ARS rating: 7.5
Performance at shows: B

| rb | pointed | large | double | 2 |

Continuity of bloom: moderate
Fragrance: slight fragrance
Growing height: tall
ARS rating: 6.9
Performance at shows: B

| ob | cupped | large | double | 2 |

Continuity of bloom: moderate
Fragrance: slight fragrance
Growing height: medium
ARS rating: 6.7
Performance at shows: B

Marijke Koopman

Mikado

Milestone

| mp | pointed | large | double | 2 |

Continuity of bloom: moderate
Fragrance: medium fragrance
Growing height: medium
ARS rating: 9.0
Performance at shows: A

| rb | pointed | medium | double | 2 |

Continuity of bloom: free and abundant
Fragrance: slight fragrance
Growing height: medium
ARS rating: 7.0
Performance at shows: A

| rb | pointed | large | double | 2 |

Continuity of bloom: moderate
Fragrance: slight fragrance
Growing height: medium
ARS rating: 7.7
Performance at shows: rarely shown

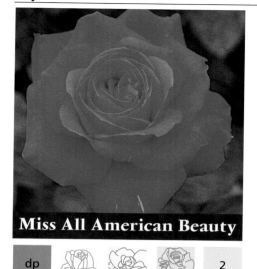

Miss All American Beauty

dp	pointed	large	double	2

Continuity of bloom:	free and abundant
Fragrance:	medium fragrance
Growing height:	medium
ARS rating:	7.4
Performance at shows:	A

Miss Canada

pb	pointed	large	double	2

Continuity of bloom:	moderate
Fragrance:	slight fragrance
Growing height:	medium
ARS rating:	7.0
Performance at shows:	B

Mister Lincoln

dr	pointed	large	double	2

Continuity of bloom:	moderate
Fragrance:	very fragrant
Growing height:	tall
ARS rating:	8.6
Performance at shows:	A

Mon Cheri

rb	pointed	large	double	2

Continuity of bloom:	somewhat "stingy"
Fragrance:	slight fragrance
Growing height:	medium
ARS rating:	6.9
Performance at shows:	A

Mrs. John Laing HP

mp	pointed	large	double	3–4

Continuity of bloom:	moderate
Fragrance:	medium fragrance
Growing height:	medium
ARS rating:	7.8
Performance at shows:	B

Mt. Hood

w	pointed	large	double	2

Continuity of bloom:	free and abundant
Fragrance:	slight fragrance
Growing height:	medium
ARS rating:	7.4
Performance at shows:	A

Norita

Oklahoma

Olympiad

| dr | pointed | large | double | 2 |

Continuity of bloom:	somewhat "stingy"
Fragrance:	slight fragrance
Growing height:	medium
ARS rating:	6.5
Performance at shows:	B

| dr | pointed | large | double | 2 |

Continuity of bloom:	moderate
Fragrance:	very fragrant
Growing height:	medium
ARS rating:	6.2
Performance at shows:	B

| mr | pointed | large | double | 2 |

Continuity of bloom:	moderate
Fragrance:	very fragrant
Growing height:	medium
ARS rating:	9.0
Performance at shows:	A

Oregold

Oriana

Papa Meilland

| dy | pointed | large |  double | 2 |

Continuity of bloom:	moderate
Fragrance:	slight fragrance
Growing height:	medium
ARS rating:	6.6
Performance at shows:	B

| rb | pointed | large | double | 2 |

Continuity of bloom:	free and abundant
Fragrance:	medium fragrance
Growing height:	medium
ARS rating:	7.4
Performance at shows:	A

| dr | pointed | large | double | 2 |

Continuity of bloom:	moderate
Fragrance:	very fragrant
Growing height:	medium
ARS rating:	7.4
Performance at shows:	A

Pascali

| w | pointed | large | double | 2 |

Continuity of bloom: moderate
Fragrance: slight fragrance
Growing height: medium
ARS rating: 8.1
Performance at shows: A

Paul Shirville

| op | pointed | large | double | 2 |

Continuity of bloom: moderate
Fragrance: medium fragrance
Growing height: medium
ARS rating: 7.4
Performance at shows: A

Peace

| yb | pointed | large | double | 2 |

Continuity of bloom: free and abundant
Fragrance: medium fragrance
Growing height: medium
ARS rating: 8.4
Performance at shows: A

Peer Gynt

| yb | pointed | large | double | 2 |

Continuity of bloom: free and abundant
Fragrance: slight fragrance
Growing height: medium
ARS rating: 6.3
Performance at shows: B

Perfect Moment

| rb | pointed | large | double | 2 |

Continuity of bloom: free and abundant
Fragrance: slight fragrance
Growing height: medium
ARS rating: 7.5
Performance at shows: B

Perfume Delight

| mp | pointed | large | double | 2 |

Continuity of bloom: moderate
Fragrance: very fragrant
Growing height: medium
ARS rating: 7.6
Performance at shows: B

Peter Frankenfeld

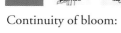

| dp | pointed | large | double | 2 |

Continuity of bloom: free and abundant
Fragrance: slight fragrance
Growing height: medium
ARS rating: 8.2
Performance at shows: A

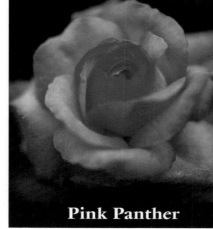

Pink Panther

| pb | pointed | large | double | 2 |

Continuity of bloom: free and abundant
Fragrance: slight fragrance
Growing height: medium
ARS rating: N
Performance at shows: rarely showed

Pink Peace

 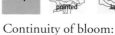

| mp | pointed | large | double | 2 |

Continuity of bloom: moderate
Fragrance: slight fragrance
Growing height: medium
ARS rating: 6.6
Performance at shows: B

Piroschka

| mp | pointed | large | double | 2 |

Continuity of bloom: moderate
Fragrance: slight fragrance
Growing height: medium
ARS rating: 7.5
Performance at shows: B

Polar Stern

| w | pointed | medium | double | 2 |

Continuity of bloom: free and abundant
Fragrance: no fragrance
Growing height: medium
ARS rating: 7.7
Performance at shows: A

Portrait

| pb | pointed | large | double | 2 |

Continuity of bloom: free and abundant
Fragrance: slight fragrance
Growing height: medium
ARS rating: 6.8
Performance at shows: B

Potton Heritage

rb | pointed | large | double | 2

Continuity of bloom: moderate
Fragrance: slight fragrance
Growing height: medium
ARS rating: 7.0
Performance at shows: A

Pristine

w | pointed | large | double | 2

Continuity of bloom: free and abundant
Fragrance: slight fragrance
Growing height: medium
ARS rating: 9.1
Performance at shows: A

Rose Gaujard

rb | pointed | large | double | 2

Continuity of bloom: moderate
Fragrance: slight fragrance
Growing height: medium
ARS rating: 8.0
Performance at shows: B

Seashell

op | camelia | large | double | 2

Continuity of bloom: moderate
Fragrance: slight fragrance
Growing height: medium
ARS rating: 6.2
Performance at shows: A

Sheer Bliss

w | pointed | large | double | 2

Continuity of bloom: free and abundant
Fragrance: slight fragrance
Growing height: medium
ARS rating: 7.8
Performance at shows: A

Sheer Elegance

op | pointed | large | double | 2

Continuity of bloom: moderate
Fragrance: slight fragrance
Growing height: medium
ARS rating: 7.7
Performance at shows: A

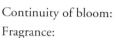

Silver Star

m	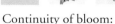			2

Continuity of bloom:	free and abundant
Fragrance:	very fragrant
Growing height:	medium
ARS rating:	7.3
Performance at shows:	B

Spaäth's Jubiläum

or				2

Continuity of bloom:	moderate
Fragrance:	slight fragrance
Growing height:	medium
ARS rating:	7.5
Performance at shows:	B

St. Patrick

yb	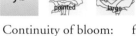			2

Continuity of bloom:	free and abundant
Fragrance:	very fragrant
Growing height:	medium
ARS rating:	7.7
Performance at shows:	A

Stephen's Big Purple

m				2

Continuity of bloom:	moderate
Fragrance:	fragrant
Growing height:	medium
ARS rating:	7.3
Performance at shows:	A

Suffolk

w				2

Continuity of bloom:	free and abundant
Fragrance:	slight fragrance
Growing height:	medium
ARS rating:	8.4
Performance at shows:	A

Tatjana

dr				2

Continuity of bloom:	free and abundant
Fragrance:	very fragrant
Growing height:	medium
ARS rating:	N
Performance at shows:	B

Tiffany

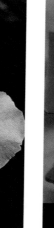

| pb | pointed | large | double | 2 |

Continuity of bloom: moderate
Fragrance: very fragrant
Growing height: tall
ARS rating: 7.3
Performance at shows: A

Timeless

| dp | pointed | large | double | 2 |

Continuity of bloom: free and abundant
Fragrance: slight fragrance
Growing height: medium
ARS rating: N
Performance at shows: A

Touch of Class

| op | pointed | large | double | 2 |

Continuity of bloom: moderate
Fragrance: slight fragrance
Growing height: medium
ARS rating: 9.3
Performance at shows: A

Tropicana

| or | pointed | large | double | 2 |

Continuity of bloom: free and abundant
Fragrance: medium fragrance
Growing height: medium
ARS rating: 7.5
Performance at shows: A

Via Mala

| w | pointed | large | double | 2 |

Continuity of bloom: moderate
Fragrance: medium fragrance
Growing height: medium
ARS rating: 7.5
Performance at shows: B

Sunset Celebration

| ab | pointed | large | double | 2 |

Continuity of bloom: free and abundant
Fragrance: slight fragrance
Growing height: medium
ARS rating: N
Performance at shows: rarely shown

Hybrid Tea

Zitronenjette

my	pointed	large	double	2

Continuity of bloom: moderate
Fragrance: very fragrant
Growing height: tall
ARS rating: N
Performance at shows: B

Polyantha

Cecile Brunner

lp	pointed	small	double	2

Continuity of bloom: free and abundant
Fragrance: medium fragrance
Growing height: medium
ARS rating: 8.2
Performance at shows: A

China Doll

mp	cupped	small	double	2

Continuity of bloom: moderate
Fragrance: slight fragrance
Growing height: short
ARS rating: 8.2
Performance at shows: B

Dick Koster

dp	cupped	small	double	2

Continuity of bloom: free and abundant
Fragrance: no fragrance
Growing height: short
ARS rating: 6.6
Performance at shows: B

Lullaby

w	flat	small	double	2

Continuity of bloom: free and abundant
Fragrance: slight fragrance
Growing height: medium
ARS rating: 8.7
Performance at shows: A

Mothersday

dr	cupped	medium	double	2

Continuity of bloom: free and abundant
Fragrance: slight fragrance
Growing height: short
ARS rating: 7.3
Performance at shows: A

Roses: A Gardener's Guide for the Plains and Prairies

Polyantha

Rugosa and Shrub

The Fairy

| lp | flat | small | double | 2 |

Continuity of bloom: free and abundant
Fragrance: no fragrance
Growing height: short
ARS rating: 8.7
Performance at shows: A

Adelaide Hoodless

| or | flat | medium | semi-double | 4 |

Continuity of bloom: free and abundant
Fragrance: slight fragrance
Growing height: tall
ARS rating: 8.8
Performance at shows: B

Altaica

| w | flat | large | single | 4 |

Continuity of bloom: spring bloom only
Fragrance: slight fragrance
Growing height: tall
ARS rating: 7.7
Performance at shows: rarely shown

Angelina

| pb | flat | medium | semi-double | 3 |

Continuity of bloom: free and abundant
Fragrance: slight fragrance
Growing height: medium
ARS rating: 7.7
Performance at shows: B

Ballerina

| mp | flat | small | single | 3 |

Continuity of bloom: free and abundant
Fragrance: slight fragrance
Growing height: medium
ARS rating: 8.8
Performance at shows: B

Belinda

| mp | cupped | medium | double | 3 |

Continuity of bloom: free and abundant
Fragrance: medium fragrance
Growing height: medium
ARS rating: 8.7
Performance at shows: B

Blanc Double de Coubert

w	ruffled	large	double	4

Continuity of bloom: moderate
Fragrance: very fragrant
Growing height: medium
ARS rating: 8.7
Performance at shows: rarely shown

Bonica

mp	cupped	medium	double	2 and 3

Continuity of bloom: free and abundant
Fragrance: slight fragrance
Growing height: medium
ARS rating: 8.5
Performance at shows: B

Cuthbert Grant

dr	cupped	large	double	4

Continuity of bloom: moderate
Fragrance: slight fragrance
Growing height: medium
ARS rating: 8.5
Performance at shows: B

Flower Carpet

dp	flat	medium	double	2

Continuity of bloom: free and abundant
Fragrance: slight fragrance
Growing height: short
ARS rating: 7.4
Performance at shows: B

George Vancouver

mr	cupped	medium	double	4

Continuity of bloom: free and abundant
Fragrance: slight fragrance
Growing height: medium
ARS rating: N
Performance at shows: B

Graham Thomas

dy	cupped	medium	double	2

Continuity of bloom: free and abundant
Fragrance: very fragrant
Growing height: medium
ARS rating: 8.4
Performance at shows: rarely shown

Grootendorst Pink

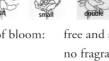

mp | flat | small | double | 4

Continuity of bloom: free and abundant
Fragrance: no fragrance
Growing height: medium
ARS rating: 7.8
Performance at shows: B

Hansa

mr | flat | large | double | 4

Continuity of bloom: free and abundant
Fragrance: very fragrant
Growing height: medium
ARS rating: 8.3
Performance at shows: B

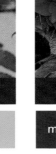

Harison's Yellow

dy | flat | small | semi-double | 4

Continuity of bloom: remontant/moderate
Fragrance: very fragrant
Growing height: tall
ARS rating: 8.2
Performance at shows: B

Hope for Humanity

dr | flat | medium | double | 4

Continuity of bloom: free and abundant
Fragrance: medium fragrance
Growing height: medium
ARS rating: N
Performance at shows: rarely shown

Jens Munk

mp | ruffled | medium | double | 4

Continuity of bloom: free and abundant
Fragrance: very fragrant
Growing height: medium
ARS rating: 9.2
Performance at shows: B

John Davis

mp | cupped | medium | double | 4

Continuity of bloom: moderate
Fragrance: very fragrant
Growing height: tall
ARS rating: 8.5
Performance at shows: rarely shown

Rugosa and Shrub

L. D. Braithwaite

    2

Continuity of bloom:	free and abundant
Fragrance:	very fragrant
Growing height:	medium
ARS rating:	7.5
Performance at shows:	rarely shown

Marie Bugnet

   4

Continuity of bloom:	free and abundant
Fragrance:	very fragrant
Growing height:	medium
ARS rating:	8.2
Performance at shows:	B

Martin Frobisher

lp 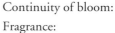 4

Continuity of bloom:	moderate
Fragrance:	very fragrant
Growing height:	tall
ARS rating:	7.2
Performance at shows:	rarely shown

Morden Centennial

mp   4

Continuity of bloom:	moderate
Fragrance:	slight fragrance
Growing height:	medium
ARS rating:	8.5
Performance at shows:	B

Morden Fireglow

mr   4

Continuity of bloom:	moderate
Fragrance:	slight fragrance
Growing height:	medium
ARS rating:	7.5
Performance at shows:	B

Morden Ruby

pb 4

Continuity of bloom:	moderate
Fragrance:	slight fragrance
Growing height:	medium
ARS rating:	7.2
Performance at shows:	rarely shown

Persian Yellow

my	 cupped	small	double	4

Continuity of bloom: spring bloom only
Fragrance: medium fragrance
Growing height: medium
ARS rating: 7.9
Performance at shows: B

Prairie Dawn

mp	cupped	medium	double	4

Continuity of bloom: free and abundant
Fragrance: slight fragrance
Growing height: tall
ARS rating: 7.5
Performance at shows: B

Prairie Joy

mp	cupped	medium	double	4

Continuity of bloom: moderate
Fragrance: slight fragrance
Growing height: medium
ARS rating: N
Performance at shows: rarely shown

Prairie Peace

yb	flat	small	single	4

Continuity of bloom: free and abundant
Fragrance: slight fragrance
Growing height: tall
ARS rating: N
Performance at shows: rarely shown

Rheinaupark

mr	camelia	medium	double	3

Continuity of bloom: free and abundant
Fragrance: slight fragrance
Growing height: medium
ARS rating: 7.8
Performance at shows: B

Sally Holmes

w	flat	medium	single	3

Continuity of bloom: moderate
Fragrance: slight fragrance
Growing height: tall
ARS rating: 8.9
Performance at shows: B

Therese Bugnet

Winchester Cathedral

Winnipeg Parks

	Therese Bugnet	Winchester Cathedral	Winnipeg Parks
Continuity of bloom:	moderate	free and abundant	free and abundant
Fragrance:	slight fragrance	very fragrant	medium fragrance
Growing height:	tall	medium	medium
ARS rating:	8.1	8.0	8.5
Performance at shows:	B	rarely shown	B

Chapter Five
Resource Material

Rose Societies

A lot of information and assistance can be obtained from the annual publications produced by many rose societies and from society members.

The larger societies also publish magazines. These manuals and magazines provide informative articles written by experts on current developments in the world of roses, and practical tips on growing and showing roses. You may also have access to their book, slide, and video library with lists of shows and rose gardens for your personal pleasure.

An international selection of interest to gardeners on the plains and prairies are:
American Rose Society
P.O. Box 30,000
Shreveport, Louisiana 71130-0030
U.S.A.
Website: http://www.ars.org/

Spokane Rose Society
42108 South Bourne Road
Latah, WA 99018-9508
U.S.A.
Phone: (206) 286-3655
e-mail: LynnsRoses@aol.com

Canadian Rose Society
10 Fairfax Crescent
Scarborough, Ontario M1L 1Z8
Canada
Phone: 416 757-8809
Website: www.mirror.org/groups/crs/

La Societe Francaise des Roses
Parc de la Tete d'Or
69459 Lyon, France
Royal National Rose Society
Chiswell Green Lane
St. Albans, Herts, England
AL2 3NR
Phone: 01727 850461

Join a Rose or Horticultural Society

At meetings and shows you meet many who are knowledgeable about rose growing. Their knowledge is helpful, especially if you are just starting to grow roses, or are new to the district. At the shows you see the roses you like the best and meet the people who grow them.

In the Spokane Rose Society publication, *Rose Ramblings*, September 1985, the editor wrote: "Smart rosarians learn by the mistakes of others. You don't have time to make all of them yourself!"

Local Rose Societies

For convenience, states and provinces with known rose societies are alphabetically listed below. However, since contact people, addresses, and telephone numbers are subject to change, we have not listed that information. Local telephone directories or the internet may provide the up-to-date information.

Alaska
Alaska Rose Society
Locations may vary

Alberta
Calgary Rose Society
Calgary, AB, Canada

Colorado
Arapahoe Rose Society,
Englewood, CO

Boulder Valley Rose Society,
Longmont, CO

Centennial Rose Society, Ft.
Collins, CO

Denver Rose Society,
Wheat Ridge, CO

Four Corners Rose Society,
Durango, CO

Loveland Rose Society,
Berthoud, CO

Montrose Rose Society,
Cedaridge, CO

Pikes Peak Rose Society,
Colorado Springs, CO

St. Vrain Rose Society,
Longmont, CO

Idaho
Idaho Rose Society,
Nampa, ID

Magic Valley Rose Society,
Twin Falls, ID

Iowa
Des Moines Rose Society
Mingo, IA

Iowa Rose Society
Ames, IA

Linn County Rose Society
Cedar Rapids, IA

Tri-City Men's Rose & Garden Club
Davenport, IA

Minnesota
Granite City Rose Society
St. Joseph, MN

Lake Superior Rose Society
Duluth, MN

Minnesota Rose Society
Maple Grove, MN

North Star Rose Society
St. Anthony, MN

Twin Cities Rose Club
St. Anthony, MN

Montana
Flathead Rose Society,
Kalispell, MT

Missoula Rose Society,
Missoula, MT

Nebraska
Beatrice Rose Society
Beatrice, NE

Crete Rose Society
Lincoln, NE

Lincoln Rose Society
Lincoln, NE

Nebraska State Rose Society
Omaha, NE

Omaha Rose Society
Omaha, NE

South Dakota
Sioux Valley Rose Society
Sioux Falls, SD

Utah
Utah Rose Society,
Bountiful, UT

Washington
Evergreen Rose Society
Lynwood, WA

Fort Vancouver Rose Society
Vancouver, WA

Grays Harbor Rose Society
Aberdeen, WA

Kitsap County Rose Society
Bremerton, WA

Lewis County Rose Society
Chehalis, WA

Lower Columbia Rose Society
Longview, WA

Olympia Rose Society
Olympia, WA

Puyallup Rose Society
Puyallup, WA

Rainy Rose Society
Kent WA

Seattle Rose Society
Seattle, WA

Skagit Valley Rose Society
Anacortes, WA

Spokane Rose Society
Spokane, WA

Tacoma Rose Society,
Tacoma, WA

Tri-City Rose Society
Richmond, WA

Tri-Valley Rose Society
Marysville, WA

Valley Rose Society
Federal Way, WA

Walla Walla Rose Society
Walla Walla, WA

Private Publication
"The Rosebank Letter"
bi-monthly by:
Rosecom
41 Outer Drive
London, Ontario N6P 1E1
Phone: (519) 652-5728
Fax: (519) 652-6850
Internet: www.mirror.org/people/
    harry.mcgee/rosebank.html

Order and Peruse the Latest Rose Catalogues

Write the rose nurseries for their catalogues and study them. They contain valuable information and many helpful suggestions.

Subscribe to the "Combined List"

This manual is published and updated annually. It lists:
- Roses in commerce and cultivation
- Rose registrations update
- Hard-to-find roses and where to find them.

Compiled and edited by Beverly R. Dobson and Peter Schneider, it may be obtained from:
Peter Schneider
P.O. Box 16035
Rocky River, Ohio 44116
U.S.A

Visit Rose Gardens

See for yourself how rose growers manage to grow their roses. Each rosarian has his own particular way of doing things and has to overcome different problems. This is the best way to learn the art of growing roses.

To encourage this idea, in 1986, the Canadian Rose Society obtained the consent of selected members throughout Canada to open their rose gardens for public viewing. The author feels honored that his rose garden had been chosen for Alberta.

In the USA, most rose societies arrange a bus tour to visit a few rose gardens during or following their rose show or convention. Each group in the bus tour is accompanied by an experienced consulting rosarian who can give sound advice on growing of roses for their particular area.

Many rose societies in the USA have established rose gardens in their cities for their members and public to learn, enjoy, and promote rose growing at large. I had the privilege of visiting these beautiful rose gardens several times in Spokane, Seattle, Portland, and California. View these gardens and those in other states. Just seeing all of these roses will likely make you want to grow them.

Importing Roses

Country-to-Country Delivery

Note: In order for roses to be shipped between Canada and the United States, the shipping nursery has to get inspected and receive a phyto-sanitary certificate from USDA, or a certificate from Agriculture Canada. This also applies to individuals who would like to send wood (cuttings, budwood) over the border. Please be aware that Canadian No. 1 Grade plants are reportedly quite a bit less mature than what American customers recognize as No. 1 Grade.

Importing to the United States

Those living in the USA who wish to import roses are advised to write for the current regulations or an import permit to:
Permit Unit
USDA, PPQ, Federal Building, Rm. 638
Hyattsville, MD 20782

This is important because the USDA regularly re-examines its policy regarding plant imports from other countries.

Current regulations prohibit importation of roses from Australia, Bulgaria, Italy, and New Zealand into the USA.

Importing to Canada

Outlined below is the proper procedure for Canadians to order rose bushes from a foreign country.
1. Obtain an "Application for Permit to Import" plants from:
   Agriculture Canada
   Plant Protection Division
   2nd Floor, West Wing, Permit Office
   59 Camelot Court, Unit R
   Nepean, Ontario.Canada K1A 0Y9
2. There are four forms to complete.
3. When completed, return the short form and #2 with a $17.00 fee

(subject to change) to the above address.

4. Send form #4 with your order to the nursery you intend to get the roses from.

5. The rose bushes will be sent in your name to the Plant Protection office nearest you for inspection. You will be advised when and where you can pick up the parcel.

Mail Order Suppliers

Carl Pallek & Son Nurseries
Box 137
Virgil, Ontario L0S 1T0 Canada
Phone: (905) 468-7262
Fax: (905) 468-5246

Corn Hill Nursery Ltd.
RR#5
Petitcodiac, New Brunswick E0A 2H0
Canada
Phone: (506) 756-3635
Fax: 800 442-3122
(Hardy roses grown from cuttings)

Hortico Inc.
723 Robson Road
R.R. 1
Waterdown, Ontario L0R 2N1
Canada
Phone: (905) 689-6984
Fax: 905 689-6566
(Co-handle Cocker's Roses, Aberdeen, Scotland)

Martin & Kraus
PO Box 12
1191 Centre Road
Carlisle, Ontario L0R 1H0
Canada
Phone: (905) 689-0230
Fax: (905) 689-1358

Mori Miniatures
PO Box 772
Virgil, Ontario L05 1T0
Canada
Phone: (905) 468-0315
Fax: (905) 468-7271

Morden Nurseries Ltd.
PO Box 1020
Morden, Manitoba R0G 1J0
Canada
Phone: (204) 822-3311

Pickering Nurseries
670 Kingston Road (Highway 2)
Pickering, Ontario L1V 1A6
Canada
Phone: (905) 839-2111
Fax: (905) 839-4807

Select Roses (Miniature Roses)
22771 - 38 Avenue
Langley, British Columbia V2Z 2G9
Canada
Phone and Fax: (604) 530-5786

The Fragrant Rose Co.
Site 41 C-3
Fanny Bay, British Columbia V0R 1W0
Canada
Phone: 888 606-7673
Fax: 250 335-1135
(a Canadian company handling Harkness Roses, England).

Arena Rose Co.
Paso Robles, California 93447
U.S.A.
Phone: (805) 227-4094
Fax: 805-227-4095

Armstrong Nurseries
PO Box 1020
Somis, California 93066
U.S.A
Phone: 1-800-321-6640

Bridges Miniature Roses
2734 Toney Road
Lawndale, North Carolina 28090
U.S.A
Phone: (704) 538-9412
Fax: (704) 538-1521

Butner's Old Mill Nursery
806 South Belt Highway
St. Joseph, Missouri, 64507
U.S.A
Phone: (816) 279-7434

Edmund's Roses
6235 S.W. Kable Road
Wilsonville, Oregon 97070
U.S.A.
Phone: (503) 682-1476
Fax: (503) 682-1275

Heirloom Old Garden Roses
24062 N.E. Riverside Drive
St. Paul, Oregon 97137
U.S.A.
Phone: (503) 538-1576
Fax: (503) 538-5902

Ingraham's Cottage Garden
370C Street, Box 126
Scotts Mills, Oregon 97375
U.S.A.
Phone: (503) 873-8610 (Antique and rare roses)

Jackson & Perkins Co.
One Rose Lane
Medford, Oregon 97501-0702
U.S.A.
Phone: 1-800-292-4769
Fax: 1-800-242-0329

Nor'East Miniature Roses Inc.
PO Box A
Rowley, Massachusetts 01969
U.S.A.
Phone: 1-800-426-6485

Regan Nursery
4268 Decote Road
Fremont, California 94555
U.S.A.
Phone: (510) 797-3222
Fax: (510) 793-5408

Richard Owen Nursery
2300 East Lincoln Street
Bloomington, Illinois 61701
U.S.A.
Phone: (309) 663-9551
(Brownell 'sub-zero' roses)

Rosehaven Nursery
8617 Tobacco Lane SE
Olympia, Washington 98503
U.S.A
Phone: (206) 456-2340

Royall River Roses
70 New Gloucester Road
North Yarmouth, Maine 04097
U.S.A.
Phone: (207) 829-5830

Sequoia Nursery (Moore Miniature Roses)
2519E Noble Avenue
Visalia, California 93292
U.S.A.
Phone: (209) 732-0309

The Conrad-Pyle Co.
372 Rose Hill Road
West Grove, Pennsylvania 19390-0904
U.S.A.
Phone: (215) 869-8011.
Wholesale only.

Bill LeGrice Roses
Groveland, Thorpe Market Road
Roughton, Norfolk, England
NR118TB

Cants of Colchester Ltd.
Nayland Road, Mile End
Colchester, Essex, England
CO45EB

David Austin Roses Ltd.
Bowling Green Lane
Albrighton, Wolverhampton, England
WV73HB
Phone: 0902-373931
Fax: 0902-372142

R. Harkness & Company Ltd.
Cambridge Road
Hitchin, Hertfordshire, England
SG40JT
Phone: 01462-420402, Fax: 01462-
422170

W. Kordes Sohne
Rosenschulen GmbH & Co KG
Rosenstrasse 54
25365 Klein Offenseth-Sparrieshoop
Germany

Useful References

All About Roses. Ortho Books. Chevron Chemical Co., Ortho Division, 575 Market Street, San Francisco, California 94105

An English Rose Garden. Thomas, Graham Stewart. Penguin Books Canada Ltd., 2801 John Street, Markham, Ontario L3R 1B1, Canada.

Be Your Own Rose Expert. Wheatcroft, Harry. Pan Britannica Industries Ltd., Waltham Cross, Herts, England

Beginner's Guide to Rose Growing. Harris, Cyril C. Sphere Books Ltd., 30132 Gray's Inn Road, London, England WC1X 8JL

Book of Roses. Home Gardens Natural Gardening Magazine. Charles Scribner's Sons, New York.

Collins Guide to Roses. Collins Park. Bertram, St. James Place, London, England.

Color Classification of Garden Roses. Canadian Rose Society, 10 Fairfax Crescent, Scarborough, Ontario, Canada M1L 1Z8

The Complete Book of Miniature Roses. Fitch, Charles Marden. Hawthorn Books Inc., 260 Madison Avenue, New York, NY 10016,U.S.A. Also Prentice-Hall of Canada Ltd., 1870 Birchmount Road, Scarborough, Ontario, Canada.

Complete Book of Roses. Krussman, Gerd. Printed in Germany in the German language. It has been translated and printed (1981), Timber Press Inc., 9999 SW Wilshire Ste. 124, Portland, Oregon 97225-9962, USA. (The best rose book the author has ever read)

Complete Book of Roses. Rockwell, F.F. The American Garden Guild Inc., and Doubleday & Company, Inc., USA

CRS Annual. Canadian Rose Society, 10 Fairfax Crescent, Scarborough, Ontario, Canada M1L 1Z8 (comes with CRS membership)

David Austin's English Roses. Austin, David. David Austin's Roses Ltd., Bowling Lane, Albrighton, Wolverhampton, England WV7 3HB

Encyclopedia of Judging and Exhibiting. Hamél, Esther Veramae. Ponderosa Publishers, Route 1, Box 68, St. Ignatius, Montana 59865 U.S.A.

Encyclopedia of Roses. An Organic Guide to Growing and Enjoying America's Favorite Flower. McKeon, Judith C., Rodale Press Inc., Emmaus, PA 18098, USA.

Encyclopedia of Roses. Taylor, George M. C. Arthur Pearson Ltd., London, England.

Everything You Wanted to Know about Pesticides for Rose Horticulture. Cairns, Thomas. Dr. Thomas Cairns, Chairman, Committee on Product Evaluation, 3053 Laurel Canyon Boulevard, Studio City, CA 91604, U.S.A.

The Facts of Light About Indoor Gardening. Staff of Ortho Books. Chevron Chemnical Company, Ortho Division, 575 Market Street, Ssan Francisco, California 94105, U.S.A.

A Family of Roses. McGredy, Sam, and Jennett, Sean. The Garden Book Club, 121 Charing Cross Road, London, England WC2W 0EB

The Gardener's Guide to Growing Roses. Matlock, John. American Rose Society.

Gardening with Roses, A Practical and Inspirational Guide. Taylor, Patrick. Timber Press Inc., 9999 SW Wilshire Ste 124, Portland, OR 97225-9962, USA.

Gardening with Roses. Taylor, Patrick. American Rose Society.

Growing Better Roses, American Rose Society, PO Box 30,00, Shreveport, LA 71130-0030, U.S.A.

Guidelines for Judging Roses American Rose Society, PO Box 30,00, · Shreveport, LA 71130-0030, U.S.A.

Guidelines to Judging Roses. Canadian Rose Society, 10 Fairfax Crescent, Scarborough, Ontario, Canada M1L 1Z8

Handbook for Selecting Roses, American Rose Society, PO Box 30,00, Shreveport, LA 71130-0030, U.S.A., ARS Annual (comes with ARS membership)

How To Grow Roses. Sunset Books and Magazines. Lane Publishing Company, Menlo Park, California, U.S.A.

Judging Roses, A Handbook for Judges, Royal National Rose Society, Bone Hill, Chiswell Green Lane, St. Albans, Herts, Herts, England AL2 3NR

Look to the Rose. McGredy, Sam. Charles Scribner's Sons, New York.

The Magic World of Roses. Bassity, A.R. Heartside Press Inc., Publishers, New York.

Modern Roses 10, American Rose Society, PO Box 30,00, Shreveport, LA 71130-0030, U.S.A.

The New Rose Book. Cavendish, Marshall. Marshall Cavendish Publications Ltd., 58 Old Compton Street, London, England W1V 5PA.

The Old Rose Advisor, Brent C. Dickerson, Timber Press Inc., 9999 SW Wilshire Ste 124, Portland, Oregon 97225-9962, USA. (A dictionary of roses, 270 color plates. A very good rose book.)

The Old Shrub Roses. Thomas, Graham Stuart. J. M. Dent and Sons Ltd., London, England.

Peter Malin's Rose Book. Malin, Peter and Graff, M.M. Brooklyn Botanic Garden, New York.

Photographic Encyclopedia. Harkness, Peter. McGraw-Hill Book Company, Maidenhead, England.

The Rose Expert. Hessayon, Dr. D. G. Transworld Publishers Ltd., 61-63 Uxbridge Road, London, England W5 58A. Also distributed by Sterline Publishing Co., 387 Park Avenue South, New York, NY 10016-8810, U.S.A., and Cavendish Books Inc., Unit 5, 801 West 1st Street, North Vancouver, British Columbia V7P 1A4.

Rose Lover's Guide, American Rose Society, PO Box 30,00, Shreveport, LA 71130-0030, U.S.A.

Roses in Color. Gibson, Michael. Orbis Publishing, London, England.

Roses, How to Select, Grow and Enjoy. MacCaskey, Michael and Ray. H.P. Books, PO Box 5367, Tucson, AZ 85703 U.S.A.

Roses, Royal National Rose Society, Bone Hill, Chiswell Green Lane, St. Albans, Herts, Herts, England AL2 3NR

Roses, Time-Life Books. Crockett, James. New York.

Roses. Hollis, Leonard. The Hamlyn Publishing Group Ltd., London, New York, Sydney, Toronto.

Roses. Kordesn, Wilhem. Studio Vista Ltd., and Blue Star House, Highgate Hill, London, England.

Roses. Phillips, Roger and Rix, Martyn. Random House of Canada, Toronto, Ontario, Canada.

Successfully Rooting Rose Cuttings, Kidger, David P. Primary Products, 100E Tower Office Park, Waburn, Massachusetts, 01801, U.S.A.

Taylor's Guide to Roses. Schneider, Peter. American Rose Society.

What Every Rose Grower Should Know, American Rose Society, PO Box 30,00, Shreveport, LA 71130-0030, U.S.A.

Winter Hardy Roses, Explorer and Parkland Series, Agriculture Canada, Publication 1922/E, Sir John Carling Building, Room 7113, Ottawa, Ontario, Canada K1A 0C7

World's Favorite Roses and How to Grow Them. Harkness, J.L. McGraw-Hill Book Company, Maidenhead, England

Super Weeder

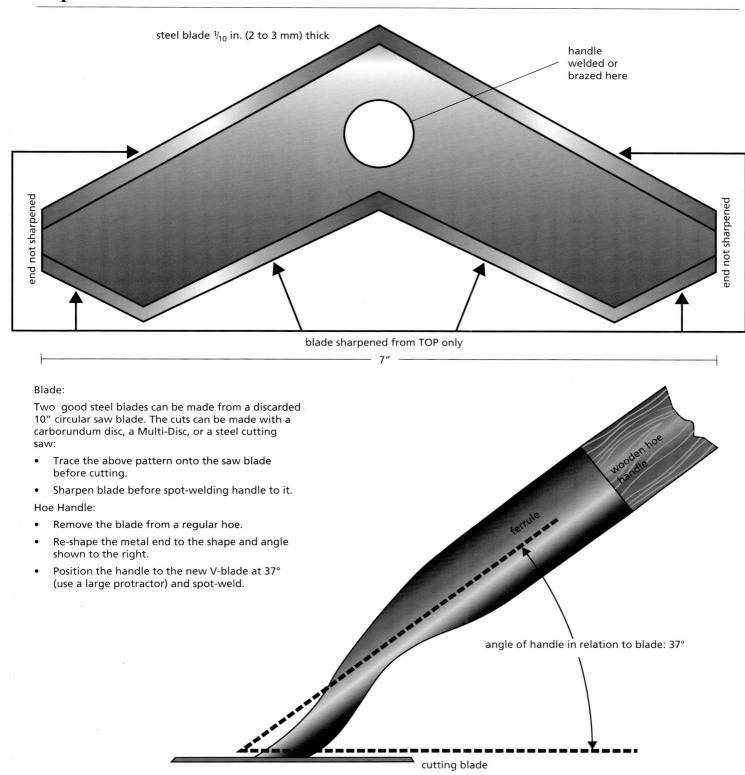

steel blade $\frac{1}{10}$ in. (2 to 3 mm) thick

handle welded or brazed here

end not sharpened

end not sharpened

blade sharpened from TOP only

7"

Blade:

Two good steel blades can be made from a discarded 10" circular saw blade. The cuts can be made with a carborundum disc, a Multi-Disc, or a steel cutting saw:

- Trace the above pattern onto the saw blade before cutting.
- Sharpen blade before spot-welding handle to it.

Hoe Handle:

- Remove the blade from a regular hoe.
- Re-shape the metal end to the shape and angle shown to the right.
- Position the handle to the new V-blade at 37° (use a large protractor) and spot-weld.

wooden hoe handle

ferrule

angle of handle in relation to blade: 37°

cutting blade

Glossary

acid soil – soil having a pH of less than 7.0.

agricultural lime – soil amendment consisting principally of calcium carbonate, and including magensium carbonate and perhaps other materials. It is used to supply calcium and magnesium as essential elements for growth of plants and to neutralize soil acidity.

alkali soil – a soil that contains enough alkali (sodium) to interfere with the growth of most crop plants usually with a pH of 8.5 or more.

alkaline soil – a soil having a pH higher than 7.0

annual – plant that completes its life cycle and dies within one year.

anther – the upper part of a stamen which holds the pollen.

artificial light – light provided by means other than the sun (e.g., fluorescent tubes, incandescent, metal halide, or high pressure sodium lamps).

balling – a condition whereby a fully developed bud fails to open.

basal break – a cane arising from a bud at the base of an old cane.

bi-color rose – a rose with two colors, where the color of the top of the petals is different from the reverse side.

biennial – a plant that produces seed during its second year of growth, after which its life ends.

blended color – two or more colors are uniformly combined.

blind end – a cane that terminates with no terminal bud.

bud – that stage of development in which the sepals are down, the petals just beginning to unfurl, and the configuration of the center is not usually evident.

bud union (graft union) – the place along the lower stem where the bud was originally budded onto the rootstock (usually visible as a slight swelling on the stem).

calyx – the outer parts of a flower called sepals, which are green in a rose.

chlorosis – a yellowing or whitening of plant tissue which may be caused by a lack of chlorophyll usually resulting from deficiencies of nitrogen, iron, or magnesium.

clay – as a particle-size term: a size fraction less than 0.002 mm in equivalent diameter, or some other limit (geologists and engineers). As a rock term: a natural, earthy, fine grained material that develops plasticity with a small amount of water. As a soil term: a textural class. As a soil separate: a material usually consisting largely of clay minerals but commonly also of amorphous free oxides and primary minerals.

clayey – containing large amounts of clay, or having properties similar to those of clay.

climber – a rose that produces long canes which require support to grow upright.

coarse texture – texture exhibited by sands, loamy sands, and sandy loams (except very fine sandy loam). A soil containing large quantities of these textural classes.

cold hardiness – condition that must be acquired by perennial plants in order to avoid injury when exposed to freezing temperatures.

compost – organic residues, or a mixture of organic residues and soil that have been piled, moistened, and allowed to decompose. Mineral fertilizers are sometimes added. If it is produced mainly from plant residue, it is often called "artificial manure" or "synthetic manure".

conditioning – a process used by florists to extend the life of a cut bloom.

confused center – refers to the petal formation in the center of the bloom; the petal arrangement lacks symmetry.

crown – the point where roots and stems join.

cultivar – a group of closely related plants propagated and cultivated from a plant with common origin and similar characteristics. Often used in place of the term variety, although varieties are usually naturally occurring selections of the species.

cultural control – prevention or control of pests using non-chemical means.

cuticle – tough, waxy covering found on the outside surface of leaves.

decorative variety – a rose suitable for garden display but lacking the excellence of bloom needed for exhibition.

desiccation – type of plant tissue injury resulting from extreme moisture loss. In continental climates, it is generally associated with low temperatures and wind.

disbudding – removal of unwanted flower buds.

disease resistance – ability of a plant to prevent the development of a disease on or in it. Resistance varies from complete immunity to slightly less than susceptible.

dormancy – plant state where growth stops. Growth usually resumes when growing conditions are more suitable.

dormancy rest – profoundly inactive state displayed by a plant during late fall and early winter. The condition is overcome following exposure to a discrete number of hours of critical low temperature. During dormancy rest, no external growth stimulus can cause active growth.

double bloom – blooms possessing more than twenty petals.

evapotranspiration – the total loss of moisture from the soil, including that by direct evaporation and that by transpiration from the surfaces of plants.

exhibition rose – a rose that when one-half to three-quarters open has classic hybrid tea form; a high center with petals symmetrically arranged in an attractive circular outline. The form may occur in many rose types, not only in hybrid teas.

fault – a defect or imperfection.

fertilizer – any organic or inorganic material of natural or synthetic origin that is added to soil to supply certain elements essential to the growth of plants.

fertilizer grade – expression of the percentage content of the fertilizer given in the order of N-P-K (nitrogen - phosphorus - potassium).

fertilizer ratio – amount of a fertilizer in relation to another or several other fertilizers (i.e., 21-14-7 indicates a ratio of 3:2:1).

floret – an individual bloom in a spray.

flower head – the collection of florets and buds that form the inflorescence.

foundation plantings – plantings at the base of a structure which tie the structure to the landscape.

friable – consistency term pertaining to the ease of crumbling of soils.

full blown – a mature, open bloom showing stamens.

fumigant – a substance used to disinfect or kill vermin.

genus (plural: genera) – a major division within a plant family. Example: all apples are of the genus Malus within the extensive Rosa family. The genus is the first part of the binomial, e.g., Malus baccata.

graft-union – point of union occurring when a shoot of one plant is grafted to the stem or root of another.

grooming – physical improvement of a specimen by the exhibitor.

hardening-off – subjecting plants to adverse conditions such as lack of moisture or nutrients in order to hasten the maturation of tissues and the proper acclimatizing of tissues to cold temperature.

hardiness – the characteristics of a plant that enables it to live through various climatic conditions, especially freezing temperatures.

heading back – type of pruning cut that is confined to stems of plants where the distal portion of the stem is removed or headed back to a lateral bud.

heeling in – a method of holding nursery plants over safely in the soil for a while until it is convenient or possible to plant.

hips – rose seed pods. Some are very ornamental. Others are often used for wine, jam, and jelly making.

host – plants from which a parasite obtains nourishment.

humus – well-decomposed part of organic matter.

hybrid – the plant that results when two different varieties or species are crossed.

hybridization – the process of creating a new plant by combining the genetic components of two separate species.

impairment – a fault or deficiency of a specimen. It may be the result of weather, poor culture, or poor grooming, or be inherent in the rose, as in the case of white streaked petals.

inflorescence – the general arrangement of flowers on an axis. An inflorescence may consist of one spray or a number of sprays.

irrigation – artificial application of water to the soil for the benefit of growing crops.

larva – immature, wingless, worm-like creature hatched from an egg which goes through minor changes to form a pupa.

lateral bud – bud located on the side of a shoot rather than at the terminal end.

leach – removal of materials in a solution. Usually done by washing out with water.

lime-induced chlorosis – failure of leaves of broad-leaved plants to produce chlorophyll when the amount of free-lime in the soil is sufficient to decrease soil acidity to the point where the availability of iron is interfered with. In clay soils having a pH above 7.6, the high lime content

may interfere with chlorophyll production. The veins usually remain dark green and the interveinal area turns yellow.

macronutrient – chemical element necessary in large amounts, usually greater than 1 ppm in the plant, for the growth of plants and usually applied artificially in fertilizer or liming materials. "Macro" refers to the quantity and not to the essentiality of the element to the plants.

matte foliage – leaves with a dull finish.

maturity – state reached by woody plants that must be achieved before tissues can be cold hardened for winter.

micronutrient – chemical element necessary in only small amounts, usually less than 1 ppm in the plant, for the growth of plants and the health of animals. "Micro" refers to the amount, and not to the essentiality of the element to the organism.

Miniature rose – a small rose plant, up to one foot (30 cm) tall with foliage and flowers in scale to height.

mulch – layer of organic or inorganic material laid on the ground to slow moisture evaporation, prevent erosion, and control weeds.

mulching – placing one of a number of materials on the soil surface.

neutral soil – soil in which the surface layer, to plow depth, is neither acid nor alkaline in reaction. It has a pH of 7.0.

nymph – juvenile insect resembling an adult which becomes an adult without an intervening pupa stage.

one-bloom-per-stem – a specimen with no side buds.

organic matter – substances derived from living things.

ovary – that part of the flower that produces the seed.

pathogens – disease-causing organisms.

peduncle (pedicel) – flower stock (stem)

perennial – plant that lives for more than two years.

perlite – heat-treated silicate rock used as a growing media.

pesticide – substance, usually synthetic, that kills or inhibits a selected type of living thing (e.g., insecticides, herbicides, fungicides, nematicides, ovicides, rodenticides, and biocides).

petiole – the stem of the leaf.

point scoring system – a means of evaluating a specimen.

pollen – contains the sperm, which fertilizes the egg within the ovary to produce seeds.

proboscis – extremely slender and sharp, pointed portion of the insects' mouth parts.

pupa – intermediate form from larva to adult.

remontant – recurrent, blooming more than once during the growing season.

rhizome – horizontal underground stem.

root house (root cellar) – a place for storing or overwintering certain plants and crops underground. Used in colder regions; the outdoor covered pit provides darkness and an even cool temperature beneath the frost line.

rootstock – stems or roots of a plant to which scions are grafted.

rosette – circular cluster of leaves or other plant organs.

sand – as a particle term: soil particle between 0.05 and 2.0 mm in diameter. As a soil term: soil textural class.

seedling – young plant that usually only contains its cotyledons or first true leaves.

semi-double bloom – blooms possessing between 12 and 20 petals.

side-dressing – method of applying fertilizer to soil surface under plants or in trenches beside plants.

silt – as a particle term: particle between 0.05 and 0.002 mm in diameter. As a soil term: textural class.

single-flowered – a bloom with one row of up to 12 petals.

soil amendment – material incorporated into the soil to make it more suitable for plant growth.

soil organic matter – organic fraction of the soil; includes plant and animal residues at various stages of decomposition, cells and tissue or soil organisms, and substances synthesized by the soil population.

soil pH – the degree of acidity or alkalinity of a soil as determined by means of a suitable electrode or indicator at a specified moisture content or soil-water ratio, and expressed in terms of the pH scale.

soil reaction – degree of acidity or alkalinity of a soil, usually expressed as a pH value.

soil salinity – amount of soluble salts in a soil, expressed in terms of electrical conductivity, percentage, parts per million, or other convenient ratios.

soil texture – proportion of sand, silt, and clay in a soil.

species – a group of roses which have one or more distinctive characteristics.

specimen – any stem terminating in a bloom or blooms. This term may be applied to Hybrid Teas, Floribundas, Grandifloras, Climbers, Miniatures, and any other type of rose, one-bloom-per-stem, or a spray.

split center – refers to the petal formation in the center of the bloom. Instead of the high, pointed center, the petals are arranged forming a cleavage resembling two or more centers.

spore – seed-like reproductive structure of fungi, ferns, and fern allies.

spray – a group of florets on one main or lateral stem. For exhibition purposes, it must show two or more blooms.

staging – tables, supports, and other items used for horticultural exhibits.

stamen – the male organ of the flower is composed of a thin stalk (filament) and a head known as the anther. The anther is the pollen-bearing organ.

stigma – the pollen receptive end of the pistil, the female part on which the pollen lands.

stock – the rooted portion of a plant in which a bud is implanted to form a new plant.

style – the stem of the pistil that joins the stigma to the ovary.

sucker – shoot arising from underground parts of a plant.

suckering – characteristics of some plants to produce new growth from adventitious buds.

systemic pesticide – herbicide, fungicide, or insecticide that is absorbed and translocated throughout the plant.

terminal bud – bud formed at the end of a shoot that normally heralds the end of extension growth for the season.

tilth – physical condition of soil as related to its ease of tillage, fitness as a seedbed, and impedance to seedling emergence and root penetration.

topsoil – layer of soil moved in cultivation. The A-horizon. Presumably fertile soil material used to topdress roadbanks, gardens, and lawns.

transpiration – release of water vapor from living tissues of the plant.

transplant – plant that is moved from one location to another. Can also denote the action of transferring a plant from one growing medium to another.

vermiculite – a sterile expanded mica medium, light brown in color, commonly used for improving the moisture and air-holding capacity of soil mixes.

water table – the level at which the soil is water saturated.

wettable powder (WP) – a pesticide in powder form that is suspended in water during application.

Index

Q

quack grass: 50, 55
Queen Elizabeth: 75
quick grass: 55
quitch: 55

R

rabbits: 56
ragweed: 55
rain gauge: 30, 62
raised bed: 5
raised beds: 24
rake: 60
ramblers: 18
rambling roses: 18, 19
rebuilding rose beds: 28
recipes: 14
recommended planting method: 26
Red Queen: 38
redroot: 52
redroot pigweed: 52, 55
rejuvenating: 37
remontant: 108
removal of unwanted flower buds: 106
removal of winter protective cover: 58
replacing rose bushes: 28
re-potting: 29
restoring wilted roses: 13
Rheinaupark: 97
rhizome: 108
rhizomes: 55
Rob Roy: 71
root ball: 28
Root barrier: 17
root cellar: 20, 25
root gall: 28
root house: 29, 59, 108
root maggot: 43
root stocks: 26
root weevil: 43
roots: 21
rootstock: 23, 108
Rosa canina: 38
Rosa multiflora: 38
Rosarium Uetersen: 66
rose
    bed: 3
    bed cover: 62
    bloom faults: 12
    bouquet: 6, 8

catalogue: 18, 101
curculio: 41
dust: 40
garden: 15, 101
grades: 22
hip jam and jelly: 14
hip vitamin source: 14
hips: 14, 107
    in a bowl: 9
    liqueur: 14
    petal tea: 14
    societies: 99, 100, 101
    mosaic: 49
    wilt: 50
    wine: 14
    as house plants: 13
    in a mixed planting: 4
    in the landscape: 3
    suitable for container growing: 5
    with pruned roots: 21
    with unpruned roots: 21
rose aphid: 43
rose arrangement: 6, 8
rose canker: 49
rose chafer: 43, 45
rose leaf beetle: 43
rose leafhopper: 43
rose rust: 49
rose scale: 43
rose slug: 43, 45
Rose Gaujard: 38, 89
rosette: 108
rough pigweed: 52
Royal Occasion (Montana): 72
rubbing alcohol: 48
rugosa cultivars: 20
Rumba: 72
run-down rose bushes: 37
rust: 30, 48, 49
rust mite: 43

S

Safers insecticidal soap: 38
salinity: 24
Sally Holmes: 97
sand: 24, 108
sandbur: 55
sandweed: 51
sandy loam: 24
Sarabande: 72

saucer: 31
saucer-like depression: 26, 27
sawdust: 25, 29, 32, 57, 58, 59
sawfly (larvae): 43
sawfly: 43
scab: 49
scale: 43
Scarlet Knight: 75
Scentimental: 72
scutch: 55
Sea Pearl: 72
Seashell: 89
secondary bud: 33
seedling: 108
selecting roses: 18
semi-double bloom: 18, 108
Senecio vulgaris: 51
Setaria viridis: 51
Sexy Rexy: 72
shade: 17, 28
shape of flowers: 20
sheep sorrel: 55
Sheer Bliss: 89
Sheer Elegance: 89
shepherd's purse: 53, 55
showing roses: 6, 11
shrub roses: 2, 4, 5, 19, 26, 57
shrub: 9, 18
side-dressing: 108
silt: 108
Silver Star: 90
Simplicity: 73
single blossoms: 18
single cut flower: 13
single stem, one bloom: 6
single-flowered: 108
size: 11
slug: 41, 44
smartweed: 55
snow cover: 19, 29, 58
soaker hose: 30
soaking roses before planting: 25
sodium chloride: 44
sodium methyldithio-carbamate: 48
soil amendment: 108
soil analysis: 24, 28
soil fertility: 24, 31
soil mix: 28, 30
soil organic matter: 108
soil pH: 108

soil reaction: 24, 108
soil salinity: 108
soil test kit: 24
soil test: 32
soil texture: 24, 108
soil: 17, 24, 25, 30
Sonchus arvensis: 54
sources of good roses: 23
sow-thistle: 55
Spaäth's Jubiläum: 90
spade: 60
species: 108
specimen: 108
Spergula arvensis: 51
Sphaerotheca pannosa: 48
spider mite damage: 45
spider mite: 19, 43, 44, 45
spittlebug: 43
split center: 12, 108
spore: 108
Spotless Gold: 47
Spotless Pink: 47
Spotless Yellow: 47
spray of floribunda roses: 9
spray: 108
sprayer: 61
spraying in hot weather: 50
spring frost: 30
sprouted roses: 22, 23, 30
spurge: 55
St. John: 73
St. Patrick: 90
staging: 6, 108
staking: 11, 36
stamen: 108
Standard Tree: 18, 20, 21
Stellaria media: 53
stem: 8, 2211, 12, 13
stem, foliage, balance, and proportion:
    10
stem pruning: 34
stem rot: 49
Stephen's Big Purple: 90
stigma: 108
stink bug: 43, 45
stinkweed: 53
stock: 108
straw covering: 58
straw: 32, 50
streptomycin: 48

style: 108
substance: 11
subterranean cutworm: 43
sucker: 36, 108
suckering: 108
sucking insect: 43
Sue Lawley: 73
Suffolk: 90
sulfate: 38
sulfur: 24, 28, 37, 58
Sun Agro: 29
sunlight: 29
Sunset Celebration: 91
Sunsprite (Korresia): 73
Super weeder: 60, 105
superphosphate: 37
support stakes: 62
sweetheart roses: 20
Sweetheart: 18
systemic pesticide: 108

T
Tabasco: 56
table salt: 44
Taraxacum officinale: 54
tarnished plant bug: 43, 45, 46
Tatjana: 90
tent caterpillar: 43
terminal bud: 108
texture: 24
The American Rose: 48
The Fairy: 36, 93
The Sun: 73
Therese Bugnet: 98
thiram: 56
Thlaspi arvense: 53
Thomomys spp: 56
three-quarters open: 10
thrips: 43, 46
Thysanoptera: 39
Tiffany: 91
tilth: 108
Timeless: 91
timing: 25
tools: 60
topsoil: 24, 108
Touch of Class: 91
trace elements: 32
transpiration: 28, 108
transplant: 28, 108

transporting roses: 13
tree bark: 32
tree roots: 17
trench: 25
Tropicana: 38, 91
Trumpeter: 74
tumble pigweed: 55
twist-tie: 12, 37, 62
two spotted spider mite: 43, 45
twitch: 55

U
useful references: 103
uses for roses: 3

V
various stages of bloom: 10
vase of roses: 6, 7
vase: 9
vegetable oil: 38
velvetleaf: 55
vermiculite: 24, 28, 30, 108
vetch: 55
Via Mala: 91
Vigor Light: 29
viral diseases: 49
Vita-Lite: 29
Viva: 74
V-troughs: 56

W
water: 38
water hose: 61
water table: 108
water wand: 61
watering: 19, 26, 30, 58
waxing: 22
webworm: 43, 45
weed control: 30
weeds: 50
weevil: 41, 43
wettable powder: 108
what roses tell you: 2
wheat straw: 58
wheelbarrow: 61
white goosefoot: 52
whitefly: 43, 45
Why grow roses?: 1
wild buckwheat: 55
wild millet: 51